Bound-for-College Guidebook

A Step-by-Step Guide to Finding and Applying to Colleges

Frank Burtnett

ROWMAN & LITTLEFIELD EDUCATION
Lanham • New York • Toronto • Plymouth, UK

Published in the United States of America
by Rowman & Littlefield Education
A Division of Rowman & Littlefield Publishers, Inc.
A wholly owned subsidary of The Rowman & Littlefield Publishing Group, Inc.
4501 Forbes Boulevard, Suite 200, Lanham, Maryland 20706
www.rowmaneducation.com

Estover Road
Plymouth PL6 7PY
United Kingdom

British Library Cataloguing in Publication Information Available

Library of Congress Cataloging-in-Publication Data

Burtnett, Frank, 1940–
    Bound-for-college guidebook : a step-by-step guide to finding and applying to colleges /
Frank Burtnett.
        p. cm.
    Includes bibliographical references.
    ISBN-13: 978-1-57886-992-3 (cloth : alk. paper)
    ISBN-10: 1-57886-992-7 (cloth : alk. paper)
    ISBN-13: 978-1-57886-994-7 (electronic)
    ISBN-10: 1-57886-994-3 (electronic)
    1. College student orientation—United States—Handbooks, manuals, etc. 2. Universities
and colleges—Admission—Handbooks, manuals, etc. I. Title.
    LB2343.32.B88 2009
    378.1'610973—dc22   2008039425

∞™The paper used in this publication meets the minimum requirements of American
National Standard for Information Sciences—Permanence of Paper for Printed Library
Materials, ANSI/NISO Z39.48-1992.
Manufactured in the United States of America.

Dedicated to my grandchildren, Jack, Alexandra and Will

Dream big dreams and then work hard to achieve them.

Contents

List of Student Exercises   vii

Introduction   ix

1   How Colleges Admit Students: Anatomy of an
Admission Decision   1
2   College Exploration: Getting Off on the Right Foot   9
3   A Calendar of Exploration, Decision-Making, and
Application Tasks   15
4   The First Step: Taking a Look at You   23
5   Mounting a Search: Getting Answers to Your College Questions   29
6   High School Course Selection: Relevance to College Admission   39
7   Learning about College Options: Getting the Best Information   43
8   Using the Internet to Explore and Apply to Colleges   51
9   Making the Most of the College Fair Experience   55
10   Campus Visits: Getting Ready to Go   59
11   Campus Visits: Being There and Afterward   65
12   Admission Plans: Modes of Admission Access   71
13   Degree of Difficulty: Understanding the
Admission Competition   75
14   College Admission Tests: Strategies for Preparation   79
15   Admission Essays: Put Forth Your Best Effort   85
16   Narrowing Options: Deciding Where to Apply   89
17   The College Application: Making It Work for You   101
18   Understanding College Costs   109
19   Types and Sources of Student Financial Aid   115
20   Making Financial Aid Forms Work for You   123
21   After the Application: What Happens Next?   129

22   Off to College: Getting Ready for Your Freshman Year   135
23   Parents and the High School-to-College Transition   143
24   Educational Success: How Counselors Can Help You   147
25   School to College: Counselors as Your Allies   149
26   Some Closing Words about Expectations   153

About the Author   155

Student Exercises

2.1	College Familiarity: Current and Future	13
3.1	Things to Do Calendar	21
4.1	Personal Characteristics Audit: Taking a Look at You	26
4.2	Setting Personal Educational and Career Goals	28
5.1	College and University Characteristics: Exploring Your Personal Preferences	33
6.1	Tracking Your High School Studies	41
7.1	Finding and Using College Guidance Resources	48
7.2	Human Information Sources: Preparing to Meet College Admission Representatives	49
8.1	Internet Sites That Help with College Exploration and Application	54
10.1	Preparing for the College Visit	62
11.1	Campus Visit Report Form: Experiences and Impressions	68
11.2	Evaluating the College Visit	70
14.1	Creating Your Admission Test Schedule	84
16.1	Examining the Admission Competition	95
16.2	Ranking the Most Important College Characteristics	96
16.3	Final Review: Creating Your Application List	97
16.4	Application List: Colleges Where You Will Submit Applications	99
17.1	The College Admission Application Checklist	106
18.1	Determining College Costs: A Personal Budgeting Process	113
19.1	Examining the Availability of Financial Aid	121
20.1	Financial Aid Application Checklist	127
21.1	From Admission to Enrollment: A Brief Checklist	133
22.1	Moving On: Packing for College	138
25.1	Tracking Counseling Sessions and Follow-up Tasks	152

Introduction

The *Bound-for-College Guidebook* contains much of the information the student who is navigating the high school to college transition needs to consider during this very challenging time in his or her life. The student will find a series of tips and suggestions about exploration, decision making, and the admission and financial aid application process. Each chapter is designed to personalize the process and educate you in becoming a better explorer, decision maker, and applicant. Understanding this information will empower you throughout the transitional process you are going to be experiencing.

Interspersed throughout the guidebook, the student will find a series of personal exercises. You will be asked to engage in personal assessment, answer questions, identify characteristics, and evaluate information that will help in the selection of your future college or university.

The product of the exercises will first be a profile of you—the future college student as seen through the characteristics that you are looking for in your future college. A by-product of completing the various exercises is the structure it will give to your college admission process. There are no right or wrong answers—simply your views, your choices, and how you think your future college will help you realize your goals. At the completion of the exercises you will have a personal portfolio to guide you through the high school to college transition.

The guidebook also contains approximately one hundred of the most frequently asked student questions (FAQs) about college admission and financial aid. Many are questions you have already raised and others represent concerns that haven't arrived on your personal radar screen yet. They are the questions that counselors and admission and financial aid professionals deal with every day and each has been answered here for you. Knowing all or most of the answers will allow you to personalize the whole process.

The process of college exploration and decision making is an evolutionary one. It will be influenced by your personal growth and maturation. The process will also be affected by the information you acquire and the ongoing experiences you have as a student. Therefore, the responses that you record here reflect a point in the process and should be reviewed and updated several times before you begin the serious task of submitting college admission applications.

Ask the people that know you (parent, counselor, teacher, or best friend) to review the student exercises you complete in this guidebook from time to time. The more they know about the value you place on the various selection criteria and the direction you are moving with your exploration, the better able they will be to guide and support you.

Your command of the information in the *Bound-for-College Guidebook* and completion of the various exercises will allow you to put the colleges you are considering to a personal test. From what you learn, you will be in a stronger position to make decisions about where to apply and where to enroll if admitted. You will also bring organization and order to your personal search, decision-making, and application activities.

CHAPTER 1

How Colleges Admit Students: Anatomy of an Admission Decision

Admission officers are charged with the responsibility of selecting students who will meet the challenges of the college or university classroom while contributing to the academic, cultural, and social climate of the institution. Different institutions place varying emphases on the criteria they employ to admit students, but the vast majority of colleges consider all or most of the following factors.

Achievement in College Preparatory Studies

A strong academic record in challenging courses throughout the high school experience will be the factor most likely to influence an admission decision in your favor. Your cumulative grade point average (GPA) and class rank (if computed by your school) will be viewed in light of the breadth and difficulty of the courses on your transcript and regarded as the best predictor of the kind of success you are likely to have in college.

ACT, SAT, and Related Test Scores

As a rule, admission tests scores alone are not likely to result in either your acceptance or rejection. Admission officers tend to view scores as a "snapshot" of the more complete person. One exception, however, is the large university that uses test scores to reduce large numbers of applications down to a manageable number for a more thorough review. Test scores may also be used for placement in some freshman classes or to award college credit for coursework considered the equivalent of the college experience.

Extracurricular Activities, Volunteerism, and Work

These experiences present a picture of the student outside of the classroom, a facet of the individual that is very important to some colleges. Activities that involve an extension of an academic endeavor (e.g., writing for the school paper) are often viewed more positively than those that are purely recreational or social (e.g., drill team). Today, many students are volunteering their time to people-oriented causes. Referenced as "service learning," these experiences are positively viewed by colleges. Involvement in some extracurricular activity is important.

Teacher and Counselor Recommendations

These firsthand observations by educators who have worked with you during your high school experience can go a long way in emphasizing your abilities, aptitudes, and interests. They often allow the writer to present information about your personality, motivation for learning, or personal philosophy that may not become known in any other way.

Essays and Writing Sample

The colleges that require a student essay consider this creative work to be an important ingredient in their admission decision. Good admission essays result from careful planning and you must allow adequate time for writing and editing.

Interview

Some colleges require or recommend a personal interview. The staff member or alumni representative conducting the interview will prepare a report that becomes an official part of the admission folder. Successful interviews require that you be yourself and display genuine interest in the college.

Special Talents and Characteristics

Any particular talent (e.g., athletic, dramatic, musical) that you have can be influential in your gaining admission to a college. You will need, however, to showcase or present those special skills to the professors, coaches, or admission officers responsible for evaluating your talents. A portfolio of your artwork or a tape of your performances can be used. Colleges may also give added consideration to members of a particular group, children of alumni or individuals with other characteristics they hope to attract.

The college or university may consider any or all of these criteria in making its admission decision. Just how much weight will be placed on a particular factor will vary from college to college. Ask an admission counselor at the colleges you're interested in attending to tell you how they make their decisions. Obtain a freshman class profile and compare your more quantifiable features (e.g., GPA, test scores) with those of admitted students. Remember, too, factors such as demographics, number of applications, and other things totally outside your control may be influential in the college's decision making.

Frequently Asked Questions

Question: Is it true that some colleges will disregard my high school's grade point average (GPA) calculation and create their own?

Answer: Yes. Many of the more selective colleges have their own criteria and formula for calculating the GPA, something they will do once they have your official transcript in hand. Less competitive institutions are more likely to use the school-generated GPA.

Question: What are my rights in the admission process?

Answer: The National Association for College Admission Counseling (NACAC), a national organization representing school and college admission counselors, has developed and refined over time a list of students' rights and responsibilities in the admission process. For example, you have the right to receive full information from each school about admission, financial aid, scholarships, and housing policies. For a copy of NACAC's *Students' Rights and Responsibilities* brochure, go to the following Internet location: www.nacacnet.org/NR/rdonlyres/FA91A978-7D6A-496A-976F-2BB5B8A53BD8/0/StudentsRtsNEW.pdf

Question: I have heard conflicting reports about how tough it is to get into college now. Just what is the competition like?

Answer: The competition for getting into colleges comes from a lot of different places. Factors such as population growth, the rise in the number of high school graduates, a greater percentage of graduates wanting to go to college, and the number of applications filed by individual applicants can individually and collectively affect the admission competition in a given year. College costs and the availability of financial aid have also caused students to "shop around" more than they once did. One thing has not changed: competition at selective institutions remains high and admission to these institutions will be granted to those presenting the strongest academic and personal qualifications.

The total undergraduate (four-year and two-year) enrollment at degree-granting institutions has been on the increase for several decades, a rise that is expected to continue for some time. Every demographic indicator leads experts to a very simple conclusion—competition for college is extremely keen at present and will continue this way for some time.

Question: How do population shifts in the United States affect the enrollment at the nation's colleges and universities?

Answer: Very dramatically. When births go up, the number of prospective college-bound students rises proportionately—even though it takes eighteen or more years for those newborns to reach the college campus. As more students earn their high school diploma, the number seeking to go on to postsecondary education increases as well. Other factors, like rising immigration numbers, have also added to the pool of prospective college-bound students. Each of these factors means increased competition for every available college desk and every dorm room.

Question: My school does not calculate class rank. Will this affect my chances of admission?

Answer: Many high schools have moved away from the policy of calculating class rank for their students and colleges have found ways of adjusting to not receiving this information. If you attend a high school that is reasonably well known by the admission officers examining your application, they will understand how your achievement compares to your fellow students and will find some method of factoring this information into their admission decision.

Question: I've been receiving unsolicited applications and information from quite a few colleges. Does this mean they are really interested in me?

Answer: In these days of direct mail marketing and wide-open Internet-driven communication tools, many colleges and universities are engaged in major information dissemination campaigns. Don't be surprised that the names of high school students are included in mass mailing lists (mail and electronic) that can be purchased by colleges. Just because you receive an unsolicited viewbook and application from a college do not assume that you are on a special list of desirable candidates. You will still need to meet the academic and personal qualifications of other competing applicants. On the other hand, if you have enjoyed a measure of academic success, especially the achievements that result in some form of award or recognition (e.g., Merit Scholar), the college materials you receive may be connected.

Question: To what extent are colleges interested in extracurricular activities and work experience?

Answer: Numerous studies of how colleges make admission decisions indicate that they look first to your current academic achievement, admission test scores, evidence of your past school performance, and potential ability to do college work. While academic credentials are the primary factors in admission, the student's involvement in activities outside the classroom can be a significant supporting factor as well. Mere membership is not important enough. It is better to show a significant level of participation or leadership in a few activities than to be superficially associated with many. Some colleges like to see extracurricular activities that are an extension of the classroom experience (e.g., science fair, debate club).

Question: My dad said that getting into a good college is nothing more than a giant "roll of the dice" in which the student has little or no control. Is he right?

Answer: Highly competitive colleges admit one student for every seven, eight, or sometimes more that apply. In that sense, the odds in favor of admission appear very competitive. You must conduct a study of the colleges where your abilities, achievements, interests, and related criteria are competitive with the students they are admitting. Let's call what you learn your AQ—your "admissibility quotient."

When you begin to match your qualifications with the profile of the student they are admitting, the pendulum begins to swing in your favor. This is where you get to exercise control by applying to colleges that are likely to accept you. Your father's reference, however, to a "good" college is somewhat troubling. There are lots of good colleges and if you look hard enough, you will discover them.

Question: The valedictorian at my school was denied admission by a prestigious college that admitted another student from our class who had lower grades. How can this happen?

Answer: It means that the college is looking for students who have something more than a high GPA to present with their application for admission. Scholarship is an incredibly important factor in college admission, but scholarship alone will not open the admission door if the college is looking for other characteristics in its rising freshman class.

Question: I attend a high school that has an extremely rigorous grading system. Will colleges take that into account when reviewing my transcript and application?

Answer: Colleges know more than you think about the high schools that send them students. While they cannot be accused of having spies in your classroom, admission officers, especially those at the more competitive colleges, make it their business to know things such as the rigor of the school's grading system. You can be sure that if it is known, it will be factored into the admission decision.

You should also know that your high school produces an annual profile to keep colleges current about grading systems, course offerings, and related information. This profile is often attached to the transcript that is forwarded in support of your application, especially if you have applied to a college outside your geographical region or the high school has not sent students to the college recently. Ask your counselor for a copy of the current profile.

Question: The media has been reporting that many colleges have altered their admission requirements to meet diversity objectives. How will this affect my application?

Answer: Many colleges have programs in place to ensure their institution attracts and educates a population of students representative of the race, ethnicity, and gender characteristics of the state, region, or nation. These programs also correct past experiences when members of minority groups and women were denied admission to college or were limited in their educational opportunities. If your application is highly competitive, you probably will not be affected in any way. If your academic abilities and achievements are less formidable, you will face stiffer competition for admission.

Question: Is it true that great grades in less challenging courses will work against me?

Answer: Great grades will never work against you. However, great grades in a sustained program of precollegiate courses are going to look even better. The more challenging the courses you take, the more influence your overall GPA will have on those making the admission decision. Consistent with your abilities, use every opportunity to select the more demanding courses. They will help you in two ways. First, they look great on your transcript, and second, the experience will prepare you for the more rigorous academic work you will encounter in college.

Question: Can I expect to be treated fairly in the college admission process?

Answer: The majority of colleges and universities in the United States subscribe to the Statement of Principles of Good Practice of the National Association for College Admission Counseling. This code of conduct has been designed by counselors and admission officers to ensure your fair treatment throughout the exploration, decision-making, and application process. It holds NACAC member institutions accountable for adherence with its standards.

Will you understand everything that is happening to you and feel that you have been treated fairly? In some instances, the answer is "no." Students denied admission to a college they really want to attend are hurt and frustrated by what they feel the college did to them. That is why it is very important to conduct a thorough investigation and discover the multiple "right" colleges for you. Don't allow your future education to be left to chance or narrow vision.

In the college admission process, you get to decide where to explore, where to apply, and where to enroll if you are accepted. The college decides who gets in. Start out by knowing what you can control and do everything in your power to make the process work on your behalf. Be flexible. Hang on to your ideals and your humor. A whole new journey is about to begin.

Question: I've heard that taking off for a year between high school and college is a "gap" year? How does this work and is it the right thing to do?

Answer: In situations like the one offered in your question, the student does exactly what she or he would do to gain admission to the choice college or university. Then, upon receiving a letter of acceptance, the student requests an enrollment deferral. You may wish to travel or have a service learning/volunteer experience during this gap year that cannot be accomplished if you are otherwise engaged as a full-time student. Reasons will vary from student to student. It's probably a good idea to offer a reason for the gap year, but increasingly students are requesting and colleges are granting these study interruptions.

Question: Is there any way to learn in advance just how colleges make their admission decisions?

Answer: Telling you exactly how they make an admission decision would be like telling you the secret recipe. It might happen—but it probably won't. Good questions, however, can provide certain insights. If you have a particular question, pose it to an admission officer or counselor. Another, somewhat trickier way to look at how colleges make admission decisions is to examine the most recent freshmen class profile for the institution. Most profiles are published and accessible by contacting the admission office. How do you compare with recent enrollees? Remember that college admission formulas are constantly in flux due to changing demographics, curricular innovations, and related factors. The best way to get the answer to your question is to be direct. Ask!

CHAPTER 2

College Exploration: Getting Off on the Right Foot

The student has an incredible amount of control in the college choice process, a factor that is not understood by some and not acted upon by others. A veteran admission officer once remarked that there are ultimately three decisions made in the college selection process, and the student gets to make two of them. The choice of where to apply and where to enroll, if accepted, are in the hands of the student. The college decides what students it wishes to admit.

The future college student must respect the power that he or she possesses in the selection process and use it wisely in order to ensure the desired outcome. Timing is a critical factor in gaining and maintaining control over the admission process. By starting early, allocating appropriate attention to all of the information-gathering, decision-making, and application-filing tasks, the student is exercising the type of control that will produce the best results.

If there is a preamble to the college selection process, it is that there is no single "right" college for you—there are many. Avoid the anguish of trying to discover "the" college that is right for you. With that bit of philosophical guidance, consider the following as you begin to explore the educational opportunities before you.

Academic Fit

Since institutions differ in the scholastic requirements they make of their students, you will want to look for colleges that "fit" you well academically. Fit means being challenged and being able to meet that challenge. Don't place yourself in an academic environment where you will simply coast for four years, and don't sentence yourself to constant pressure about whether you're going to succeed. Academic fit should be your number one criteria in the selection of a college.

Environmental Fit

Choosing a college is very much like looking for a new home. The truth is that a college campus is going to be your home for a significant portion of the next two, four, or more years. Try to find an environment where you will feel comfortable as a citizen; a place that presents the social, cultural, and lifestyle comforts that you desire. Don't go looking for Utopia University. It probably doesn't exist. The important element here is to look for things you want and things you want to avoid. When you find the right balance in those elements, you probably have found colleges worthy of a closer look.

Affordability

The cost of college today cannot be dismissed as a factor in the selection process, but students and parents should attempt to separate, to the extent possible, financial issues from the academic and social factors. There was a time when the affordability issues were only a concern of the poor. Upward of two-thirds of the student body at some colleges are utilizing some form of financial aid.

Today, the financial concern casts a shadow across many families in many different economic categories. Before dismissing a college or university from consideration in the exploration process, the student should gather information about the availability of all forms of financial aid. When all financial aid options are considered, some institutions, which first appear unaffordable, may, in fact, be more reasonably priced than others.

Your initial journey into college exploration can be an exciting time in your life . . . part of that "coming of age" that your parents, teachers, and other adults often talk about. Avoid the anxiety and discomfort that some students experience during this time by setting a course that is characterized by good planning and the use of all of the resources at your disposal.

If you have engaged in thorough examination of your abilities, aptitudes, goals, and interests, the chances are very likely that you will apply to colleges that will meet your needs, ones that will offer you the opportunity to continue to grow academically and socially. Enjoy the journey!

Frequently Asked Questions

Question: Do you have any general advice to offer about managing the whole college admission process?

Answer: Two issues come to mind immediately. Give yourself sufficient time to do what needs to be done and remain organized throughout the experience. The time part will be explained in calendars that appear later in this guidebook and the presentation of tasks that you need to perform in a certain order. The organization part is, for some, more difficult. You are going to be collecting a lot of information and making a lot of notes and generating a lot of "stuff" during this process. Create a college-planning portfolio. A savvy counselor once referenced the old adage: "A place for everything and everything in its place" when recommending the creation of a college-planning portfolio. You'd be wise to follow that guidance.

Question: As I examine prospective colleges, what should I be looking for?

Answer: Different students will apply different criteria to their examination. Your primary goal is to find the best possible place for you to learn. In addition, you want to study in an academic and social environment that is comfortable for you. Conduct a personal audit of all of the things that are important to you and then apply those criteria to all the colleges and universities you encounter in your search.

That "different strokes for different folks" maxim certainly can be applied here. You might place a lot of importance on academic reputation of the college, availability of a major field of study, whether it has a lacrosse team, or how close it is to home. Your best friend, on the other hand, may be more interested in the success rate that graduates have in the work world, size, or type of community in which it is located.

Determine first the things that are important to you and then go about looking for colleges that have those characteristics. Remember, you're looking for the place where you are going to be learning and living for the next four or more years. Be thorough and you will most likely be successful.

Question: I've heard lots of "right" reasons for choosing a college. What are the wrong reasons?

Answer: There are many "wrong" reasons for selecting a college. The first that comes to mind is giving up control of the decision-making process and letting family or friends, even teachers and counselors, tell you the best place to go to college, and then doing exactly what they say. It's your life and your decision, and you need to keep control of both. Another common error is examining colleges based solely on cost. While cost is a very important element in the exploration and decision-making process, your primary concern should be with whether the college is the right place to both live and learn. If these conditions are not present, your chances of succeeding are at risk and the cost probably won't matter much.

Question: What are the advantages of attending a community college?

Answer: Community college enrollment grew dramatically over the past twenty years because these institutions filled a vital education need of the nation. Many of the educational programs taught at the two-year level respond directly to the career objectives of their students. Second, community colleges allow developing students to continue their education (full- or part-time) and then transfer to a four-year college or university. Because community colleges are local and publicly supported, they also provide an affordable alternative for many students. Whether you are interested in obtaining a two-year associate's degree or just taking a refresher course in a particular subject, the community college is worthy of your full consideration.

Question: What are school-to-work programs?

Answer: The term "school to work" is used to describe programs that help ease a high school student's transition from the classroom into the working world. Typically, students in these programs take courses part of the day and then work in a business that relates to their interests. The School-to-Work Opportunities Act, signed into law in 1994, funds efforts by parents, teachers, and business leaders to better prepare students for the world of work. Find out if there are school-to-work opportunities for you in your school or school district and then determine if one is right for you.

Student Exercise 2.1

COLLEGE FAMILIARITY: CURRENT AND FUTURE

1. In the spaces below list the colleges and universities with which you have *some level of familiarity*, but ones that you wish to examine in greater detail as you proceed through the exploration process:

_____	_____
_____	_____
_____	_____
_____	_____
_____	_____

2. In the spaces below list the colleges and universities with which you have *little or no familiarity*, ones that you will need to examine thoroughly as you proceed through the exploration process:

_____	_____
_____	_____
_____	_____
_____	_____
_____	_____

CHAPTER 3

A Calendar of Exploration, Decision-Making, and Application Tasks

In order to move progressively through the exploration, decision-making, and application process, the student needs to avoid the two Ps—pressure and procrastination. Pressure is self-inflicted when tasks are not completed according to required timetables. Such failure can have devastating results, especially when the task not completed on time is filing the application for admission or financial aid. The other enemy is procrastination—putting off until later what needs to be done now. Procrastination can lead to the pressure that many students feel throughout the process.

Most tasks are known and capable of being placed on a schedule of "things to do." Following is a year by year listing of some of the more significant tasks.

Sophomore Year

Success in the school-to-college transition may be measured in how well you address the responsibilities that are associated with becoming a good student, most notably the development of strong academic skills. This begins early in the high school experience. Develop the ability to study and learn, and the result will be the kind of academic achievement that will enhance your future education options.

1. Meet with your counselor to review your program of studies in relation to the graduation requirements and the general requirements for admission to college. Conduct this audit within the context of a four-year high school plan and make certain that your current courses are reflective of where your abilities and interests suggest you should be in your sophomore year.

2. Talk with your teachers, counselor, and parents about your personal skills and competencies as a student. Identify your strengths and the areas that could be strengthened. Seize every opportunity to learn and practice study skills and habits such as note taking, time management, keyboard training, and reading efficiency.

3. Arrange to take a career aptitude test and/or interest inventory. These tools will identify possible fields for you to consider as you move through high school and consider future educational and career options. Your counselor can suggest the appropriate tests and help you to interpret the findings.

4. Learn what you need to know about the various tests that may be required or used in the college admission process (including test dates, times, and sites): PLAN® (preliminary test for the ACT assessment) and/or Preliminary SAT/National Merit Scholarship Qualifying Test (preliminary test for the SAT I: Reasoning Test). As you complete certain academic studies, you may wish to take the SAT Subject Test in that area. If you possess a particular academic ability and interest, you should also consider participation in Advanced Placement (AP) courses and eventually take the appropriate AP examination. Review the results of each test that you take with your counselor.

5. Begin the process of self-awareness, the ongoing activity in which you analyze your aptitudes, achievements, interests, and goals.

6. Determine what tools (computerized guidance information systems) and resources (guides, viewbooks, videos) are available in your school's college and career resource center, guidance office, or library to assist you in exploring colleges. Start your exploration with the print information found in the general guides. Advance to the specific information that colleges offer prospective students at their Internet websites. These resources, along with your counselor, teachers, and others, will become your information allies over the next two or three years.

7. Learn how to use the informational tools and resources of the school and community library. See if any college libraries in your community can offer you similar exposure.

8. Set aside some time in your personal schedule to engage in leisure reading, practice your computer keyboard skills, or participate in sports and activities away from the classroom. Most colleges want to admit the "well-rounded" person, but some students can go overboard. Become engaged in one or two extracurricular activities rather than spread thinly across many.

9. Study hard and maximize every learning opportunity available to you. You'll thank yourself in a couple of years.

A sound sophomore year will provide the foundation for a first-rate high school experience. Moreover, the habits and skills you acquire early on will serve you through high school, college, and on into the career world.

Junior Year

You've reached the middle of your high school experience. While college may seem like it is way off in the future somewhere, your junior year is the time to give more structure to your exploration so that you fully match your educational achievements, aptitudes, and interests with all viable options. Consider the following activities:

1. Continue to apply yourself in the classroom. Junior courses, especially those in a college preparatory curriculum, are more intensive and teachers may be expecting more of you. However, the academic and personal skills that you are now learning to master will serve you for a lifetime, and are essential for success in college.
2. Meet again with your counselor to review your academic schedule and the progress you're making. As you begin to create the list of colleges that interest you, compare your academic profile with the specific admission requirements at those institutions. Remember that admission officers see many applications from prospective students that meet their requirements. Therefore, your best chances for admission will be if you surpass the basic requirements.
3. Schedule and take the ACT, SAT, or any related standardized tests that you and your counselor determine may be required for admission to college. Participate in any test prep classes that may be available through your school or community organizations or available via fee-charging commercial services. Review the results of any preliminary tests that you have taken and schedule the next round of tests. Consult with your teachers and counselor about how you might improve your test scores. Continue to take subject tests and Advanced Placement exams as you complete the appropriate courses.
4. Mount a serious information-gathering campaign, one that allows you to match prospective colleges to your personal abilities, achievements, interests, and learning objectives. College guides and viewbooks are an excellent way to initiate your research. Then step up to the more specific information that colleges present about admission and financial aid on their websites. Take advantage of computerized guidance information programs and college videotapes in the guidance department or library. Attend college fairs and special seminars offered by counselors to disseminate information about the admission and financial aid processes and assist in completing applications.
5. Arrange a personal meeting with your counselor to get the individual attention that you might need to gather information and consider educational options after high school. Your counselor can direct you to appropriate resources and then assist in the evaluation and use of the information you have acquired.

6. Try to visit the colleges that are at the top of your interest list. Arrange to tour the campus, sit in on a class, attend a concert or athletic event, and meet with admission counselors to get the answers to your specific questions and learn more about each institution. Make every attempt to visit colleges when they are in session. Stay in a dorm if permissible. Look around the city or community in which the college is located. Continue your campus visits into the summer and on into the fall of your senior year.

7. Interact regularly with your parents to keep them informed about where your exploration is taking you and allow them to track your progress and define ways in which they can be supportive. Encourage them to read the guides and viewbooks, accompany you to college fairs and campus visits, and participate in counseling programs designed for parents.

8. Begin the process of refining your list and learn as much as you can about these colleges. It will soon be time to identify a final list of colleges where you will file applications.

9. Consider using the summer between your junior and senior year to enroll in a class at a local college or to participate in a special seminar (e.g., creative writing, keyboard training). Otherwise, work at a summer job, relax, and prepare for that final year.

Can you believe it? Only your senior year stands between you and the college experience. You continue to evolve and grow as an individual as do the expectations that your parents, teachers, and others have of you. Get ready! Your senior year lies just ahead.

Senior Year

You're in the countdown year—the final year of high school. In just a short time you will be making final decisions and applying for admission to college. It will be a very exciting and busy year, a time for you to address the following tasks:

1. Refine or reduce the list of colleges you have under consideration to a manageable number. For most, it will be a number up to three—for others three to five—and for some, five or more. There is no magic number! Keep colleges on the list that you are really interested in attending. Locate the admission and financial aid forms for your narrowing list on the various college websites. A great many colleges will give you the option of completing and submitting these forms online. Others will let you complete the forms online, which you can print and send via regular mail. Elect whatever admission application submission action is most comfortable for you.

2. Meet once again with your counselor to review your academic record and current courses in light of the list of schools where you want to file applications. Arrange to have a current (and eventually final) transcript of your grades forwarded to these colleges where this official school document will become a part of your admission application.

3. Determine what admission, achievement, and related tests you will need to take during the coming months and register immediately. Consult with your counselor regarding the benefits of repeating one or more of these examinations. If you are seeking collegiate credit for Advanced Placement courses, then be sure to register and complete the appropriate AP tests.

4. As you begin to review the admission applications and financial aid forms, create a checklist and calendar for each important milestone and deadline. Note that applications for early decision and early action must be filed much earlier. Review and update your checklist on a regular basis. Earlier in this guidebook the suggestion of creating a college planning portfolio was offered. As you narrow your list of colleges where you intend to make application, having a "file within a file" for each application makes a great deal of sense.

5. If you will be applying for any type of financial aid, you will need to acquire and complete the Free Application for Federal Student Aid (FAFSA). Some colleges will require that you submit the CSS/Financial Aid PROFILE® and/or their institutional aid application. Your counselor will have copies or you can find them on the Internet. Check deadlines for state aid programs and file forms accordingly.

6. Set aside some time for the orderly completion of college applications and forms. Pass along any teacher and counselor recommendations that must be completed in support of your application. This process should begin in mid- to late October. Note that some colleges will request an essay or writing sample. Address this task early so that it receives the necessary attention. If you are applying for private scholarships or participating in academic competitions, be aware of their requirements and deadlines.

7. Continue to communicate with your counselor. Your school will be required to send an official transcript of your academic record and related information to the college(s). Once you are certain that you are going to make application, forward the appropriate forms to your counselor.

8. Continue to devote the required attention to your senior classes. Your acceptance at any college will be conditional upon the satisfactory completion of your senior classes. Don't slack off!

9. If you have applied to more than one college, rank your preferences so that you can address multiple acceptances when colleges inform you of their admission decision. Your decision can be complicated by placement on the wait-list at a particular college. If you are not accepted at any of the college(s)

where you have applied, a visit to your counselor will allow you to review your options.

10. Once you have made your final decision about where to enroll, send your deposit, housing forms, and related materials. Review the freshman orientation packets and college course selection forms as they are received. Say "thank you" to everyone that helped you.

Finally, take a bit of time to consider what you have accomplished and be proud that you are about to enter a new phase of your life . . . the world of a college freshman.

Frequently Asked Questions

Question: Even if I maintain an orderly schedule for gathering information and completing the tasks associated with the various calendars, how will I know that I am on track?

Answer: At the beginning of the college exploration process, you "don't know what you don't know." With each step of the exploration and decision-making process, additional information will be revealed. Many of your questions will be answered. Information can also generate new questions. Your sophomore inquiry will be somewhat general, followed by a more learned and targeted inquiry in your junior year. The senior and application year is far more focused. Get behind and you lose valuable control.

Student Exercise 3.1

THINGS TO DO CALENDAR

Review the tasks in the sections that preceded this exercise and make a personal list of "things to do" as you proceed through the exploration, decision-making, and application processes. Note each task on the calendar and check it or cross it off when completed.

Sophomore Year Tasks   **Completed**

_____

_____

_____

_____

Junior Year Tasks   **Completed**

_____

_____

_____

_____

_____

_____

Senior Year Tasks   **Completed**

_____

_____

_____

_____

_____

_____

CHAPTER 4

The First Step: Taking a Look at You

As you embark on your study of educational options, it is important to begin by taking a long, hard look at yourself. Who are you? What are your likes and dislikes? What do you consider your academic strengths and weaknesses? And maybe the most important question— why are you going to college?

By gaining a full understanding of yourself, you can personalize the entire college exploration and selection process. When it comes time to make decisions, you'll be making them in full consideration of the person that will be called upon to implement them—you!

During childhood and adolescence, you have no doubt become aware of the individual characteristics that you possess that are similar to and different from your peers. These characteristics include aptitudes, achievements, interests, personality traits, values, and goals: elements that will impact your educational and career development.

Awareness of these characteristics will allow you to make decisions that are consistent with your individuality. Failure to conduct periodic audits of these traits is an error that can have significant consequences on your future success.

Aptitudes represent your capacity for learning, your natural ability to do something. When someone makes the statement, "He's/she's a natural," when referring to one's ability in music, athletics, or some other area of endeavor, they are really speaking of his or her exceptional aptitude in these areas. Others may have an aptitude or unusual capacity for learning in science, mathematics, writing, or other studies.

Achievements are the measured accomplishments in your life, those things that you have done well. In school, progress is measured regularly and reported to you in the form of grades or academic awards. In athletics, performances are measured by a stopwatch or statistics. In music, art, or theater, your achievements may result in recognition or praise for a job well done. It is possible to achieve or become accomplished in something for which you have little or limited aptitude. This is usually the result of concentration and hard work.

Interests are the things you like to do, commanding your time and arousing your curiosity. Sometimes, interests are spin-offs of your aptitudes and achievements as they represent areas where you have devoted study and attention and earned some degree of success. Other interests are outlets or diversions, things you do simply for fun.

Personality traits are those characteristics that make one person different from another. In psychology, personality is defined as the total physical, intellectual, and emotional structure of a person, including his or her aptitudes, abilities, and interests. Words like *outgoing, quiet, inquisitive,* and *intellectual* are often used to describe people. Knowing your own personality traits can help you define educational and career environments that are conducive to the person that you are.

Values are the aspects of your life that you hold in esteem, things you would prefer if you had a choice. They are the principles or ideals that you stand behind. A sense of self-awareness would be incomplete without some analysis of the values you possess and how they relate to your development. For example, prestige and status may be important to you, but mean less to a classmate.

Goals represent what you hope to accomplish in the future. Have you ever stopped and asked why you're going to college? The response should not be that everyone else is going. The real answer, in part, represents your educational goal and may be tied to your long-term career goal. While some students have definite educational and career objectives, others may be less exact. Some simply choose to go to college to grow intellectually. Others want to learn about things that interest them. Still others are seeking the knowledge and skills that will launch them into their chosen career. The more your college choice allows you to move toward the realization of your goals, the more satisfying the experience may be for you personally.

Students have a greater chance of succeeding in their educational pursuits if they find a learning and living environment that is compatible with and supportive of their aptitudes, achievements, interests, personality traits, and values, one that will assist them in realizing their educational goals.

Frequently Asked Questions

Question: I'm trying to decide if I really want to go to college? Will a degree make a difference in my future earning power?

Answer: Studies conducted by the U.S. Department of Labor's Bureau of Labor Statistics and the U.S. Census Bureau give meaning to the theory that "the more you learn—the more you earn." Following are recent median annual income levels by educational attainment: less than high school—$21,447, high school diploma—$33,265, associate's degree—$35,401, bachelor's degree—$46,300, master's degree—$55,300, and advanced graduate/professional (doctorate, medicine, law, etc.) degree—$70,500. Another important thing to note: Unemployment rates go down for persons as their educational attainment rates go up.

Question: If I haven't made a final career decision, how can I choose a college that's right for me?

Answer: Relax. Your final career decision can follow your college decision. If you have some idea of what you want to do (e.g., engineering, business, communications), you can use your collegiate studies to validate that interest. You may need to consider colleges that allow you the flexibility to continue your exploration. If you have absolutely no idea as to your future career, look for a college where you can use the first couple of years to get some of the basic degree requirements completed while you continue the process of career exploration and discovery. Remember, too, the value associated with learning to learn. There is a lot to be said for studying for the enrichment of life and allowing your career ambitions to fall into place later.

If you want to engage in more intensive career exploration at this time, talk to your counselor about taking a career interest inventory and consider getting some hands-on experiences in the work world to see if any occupation or career field begins to appeal to you.

Question: Is it bad to list my major as "undecided" on my application if asked?

Answer: In a perfect world, every college applicant would know what he or she wanted to study in college and do in a future career. But, we all know how imperfect this world happens to be. You may still be in the process of discovering your abilities, aptitudes, and interests and linking these characteristics with future career and lifestyle preferences. For many, this will continue throughout your young adult years. It is perfectly acceptable to indicate "undecided" on your application. In fact, undecided is one of the more popular majors of incoming freshmen at many colleges.

Student Exercise 4.1

PERSONAL CHARACTERISTICS AUDIT: TAKING A LOOK AT YOU

Complete the answers to the following questions. Review your answers periodically and update any information that does not reflect your current view of your personal characteristics.

1. Make a list of five adjectives you feel your friends/fellow students and teachers/counselor would use to describe you:

Friends/fellow students: Teachers/counselor:

1. _____   1. _____
2. _____   2. _____
3. _____   3. _____
4. _____   4. _____
5. _____   5. _____

2. Make a list of five adjectives you would use to describe yourself:

1. _____
2. _____
3. _____
4. _____
5. _____

3. What do you consider to be your greatest personal strengths or attributes?

_____
_____
_____
_____

4. What do you consider to be your greatest weaknesses or shortcomings?

_____
_____
_____
_____

5. List three academic subjects or interests you would like to continue to study:

   1. _____

   2. _____

   3. _____

6. Which high school courses have you enjoyed the most?

   _____

   _____

   _____

   _____

   _____

7. Which high school courses have posed the most difficulty?

   _____

   _____

   _____

   _____

   _____

8. Identify a recent experience (school or nonschool) that stimulated your intellectual curiosity:

   _____

   _____

   _____

   _____

   _____

9. How would you describe your academic performance to date? Is your high school record a true reflection of your academic ability and potential? If not, how would you characterize your ability and potential to succeed in college?

   _____

   _____

   _____

   _____

   _____

Student Exercise 4.2

SETTING PERSONAL EDUCATIONAL AND CAREER GOALS

1. What is your immediate educational goal? Why are you going to college or on to postsecondary education?

_____

_____

_____

2. What would you like to study? Have you decided on a college major or specific program of study?

_____

_____

_____

3. What is your eventual educational goal (e.g., bachelor's degree, master's, etc.)?

_____

_____

_____

4. Have you set a career goal or identified a field (e.g., business, communication, health, public service, etc.) in which you would like to work? If yes, what is that occupation or field?

_____

_____

_____

5. To what extent is your college choice relevant to your career goals?

_____

_____

_____

6. What do you consider to be your strongest academic (e.g., writing, computation, analytical) skills? To what extent do you wish to pursue collegiate studies related to these skills?

_____

_____

_____

CHAPTER 5

Mounting a Search: Getting Answers to Your College Questions

During the exploration process the student will have an opportunity to ask a lot of questions in order to find the colleges that meet the academic, environmental, and financial requirements that he or she has established as important. The decision whether to apply to a college will be tied directly to the information that is collected and the impressions that are made during this evaluative process.

Following are a number of questions that you, the student, should ask as part of this exploration. The list should not be viewed as exhaustive (you will certainly think of others), and they are not presented in any kind of priority order.

Program of Study, Academic Philosophy, Reputation

Does the college offer the academic specialty you wish to pursue? What is the academic reputation of the institution in general and the program (e.g., journalism, engineering) in particular? Do graduates get good jobs and are they admitted to grad school? Does the college have a strong library and use the latest tools and technology to educate its students? What are the requirements for success in the classroom? Does the institution ascribe to a particular philosophy of teaching or learning? What is the typical class size? Do the best professors teach classes at the undergraduate level?

Admission Requirements and Competition

How will your abilities, aptitudes, and previous achievements stack up against other applicants and enrolled students? How have students with your academic credentials fared in the admission process? What is the profile of the typical student at the college? What percentage of admitted students graduate? In how many years? What success do graduates have in finding jobs and gaining admission to graduate school?

Location and Setting

Are you interested in going to a college nearby, in the state or region, or anywhere in the United States or the world? Do you have a preference to the type of community (e.g., large city, small city, rural) where the college is located? How important is the campus setting (e.g., open spaces and tree-filled lawns versus high-rise buildings)?

Institutional Characteristics

What type of institution best suits your academic and environmental needs? Do you prefer a large university with multiple academic venues, a small liberal arts college, or something in between? Do you want to study at a two-year or four-year college? Do you prefer a public or private, coeducational or single-sex, church-affiliated, or career-oriented institution?

Accommodations

Are the dormitories comfortable and well furnished? Will the food service respond to your dietary needs? Can your physical fitness and recreational interests be satisfied? Is living on campus mandatory? What percentage of students live off campus?

Social, Cultural, Extracurricular Atmosphere

What social, cultural, and leisure time opportunities are available? Do you have interests outside of the classroom (e.g., music, sports, drama, volunteerism) that you would like to maintain while in college? If so, will the college or the community allow you to pursue those interests? Is there a church, synagogue, mosque, or other related congregation on campus or in the community that will satisfy your faith-based interests?

Special Needs or Considerations

Can the college respond to tutorial, counseling, health, or other special needs that you might have? Does the campus and surrounding community present a secure living environment?

Cost

What is the cost of tuition, room and board, and other fees? What personal (e.g., transportation) costs will be required? What financial aid opportunities exist, and what are the qualifications? Is financial need factored into the admission decision? Are there opportunities for part-time work on campus or in the community?

It will be next to impossible to find any college that gets a five star rating in each of these areas of exploration. In the final analysis, does the college present you with a good feeling? Is it a place where you see yourself learning and living over the next four or more years? If the answer is "yes," the next step is to get an application for admission.

Frequently Asked Questions

Question: How can I determine the particular reputation of a school or department within a college that I'm considering?

Answer: You've hit upon one of the problems associated with "rating" and "ranking" guides. Often there are exemplary departments within less than exemplary institutions. These may be overlooked if the student goes only by the general reputation of the college or university. Sometimes national professional associations accredit study programs, and career entry may be limited if you fail to get your degree from an accredited institution. Ask someone currently in the profession if such an accreditation program exists.

Otherwise, the best barometer may be the impressions of recent graduates or those students currently enrolled in the program of study. The answer to a question as simple as "do graduates find employment in their career field" or "do graduates gain admission to graduate school" can tell you a great deal about the reputation of the department or school.

Question: Will I be taught by professors or teaching assistants? How can I find out?

Answer: You've probably heard that the best professors at some colleges are only teaching graduate classes or are devoting their academic time to research, writing, and related scholarly work. Unfortunately for you, this may be the case. In response to the increasing number of times they are being asked this question, many colleges are making available information regarding the number and/or percentage of undergraduate classes that are taught by professors versus those taught by teaching assistants. You can ask the admission office for this information. But don't be totally turned off by teaching assistants. This work is viewed somewhat like an apprenticeship and many assistants are doing excellent teaching at the nation's colleges.

Student Exercise 5.1

COLLEGE AND UNIVERSITY CHARACTERISTICS: EXPLORING YOUR PERSONAL PREFERENCES

Listed below are the characteristics most students look for when selecting a college. **Review the entire list of criteria and then go back and evaluate each according to their importance.** *Very Important* means the characteristic will weigh heavily in your future evaluation of the college. *Somewhat Important* suggests the presence of this characteristic would enhance your future consideration of the college. *Not Important* means the characteristic will have no bearing on or does not apply to your consideration of colleges at this time.

These characteristics should not be viewed as an exhaustive list. You may have other or more specific items that you would like to see present in the colleges that you are considering. Use the blank spaces found at various points on the profile to insert these personal exploration characteristics.

Exploration Criteria	Very Important	Somewhat Important	Not Important
1. Academic Reputation			
a. General reputation of the college	_____	_____	_____
b. Specific reputation of the major or program of study	_____	_____	_____
2. Curriculum or Program of Study			
a. Availability of the major or specific program of study I want to study	_____	_____	_____
b. Availability of first-rate general or liberal arts curriculum	_____	_____	_____
3. Academic Support Services			
a. Availability of special services (e.g., tutoring, advising, etc.). List requirements below:			
b. _____	_____	_____	_____
c. _____	_____	_____	_____
d. _____	_____	_____	_____

Exploration Criteria	Very Important	Somewhat Important	Not Important
4. Academic Philosophy and Instructional Style			
a. Class size	_____	_____	_____
b. Undergraduate access to experienced professors and teachers	_____	_____	_____
c. _____	_____	_____	_____
5. Type or Affiliation of Institution			
a. Public	_____	_____	_____
b. Private	_____	_____	_____
c. Special focus (e.g., career training)	_____	_____	_____
d. Two year	_____	_____	_____
e. Four year	_____	_____	_____
f. Single sex	_____	_____	_____
g. Coeducational	_____	_____	_____
h. Historically black college/ university	_____	_____	_____
i. Religious affiliation	_____	_____	_____
j. Military affiliation	_____	_____	_____
k. _____	_____	_____	_____
l. _____	_____	_____	_____
6. Academic and Related Facilities			
a. Classrooms and lecture facilities	_____	_____	_____
b. Computer labs and facilities	_____	_____	_____
c. Science labs and facilities	_____	_____	_____
d. Library and research facilities	_____	_____	_____
e. Telecommunication facilities	_____	_____	_____
f. _____	_____	_____	_____
g. _____	_____	_____	_____

Exploration Criteria	Very Important	Somewhat Important	Not Important
7. Retention, Graduation, and Placement Rates			
a. Freshmen students returning for sophomore year	_____	_____	_____
b. Graduation rate of entering students	_____	_____	_____
c. Career placement success of graduates	_____	_____	_____
d. Graduate and professional school placement success of graduates	_____	_____	_____
e. _____	_____	_____	_____
8. Size of Undergraduate Student Population			
a. Large student body (7,500+)	_____	_____	_____
b. 5,000–7,499 students	_____	_____	_____
c. 2,500–4,999 students	_____	_____	_____
d. 1,000–2,499 students	_____	_____	_____
e. Small student body (under 1,000)	_____	_____	_____
f. _____	_____	_____	_____
g. _____	_____	_____	_____
9. Location			
a. Anywhere in the United States	_____	_____	_____
b. Anywhere in the region (multistate)	_____	_____	_____
c. Anywhere in the state	_____	_____	_____
d. Immediate area (75–100 miles)	_____	_____	_____
e. Within commuting distance	_____	_____	_____
f. Specific location (insert below):			
_____	_____	_____	_____
_____	_____	_____	_____

Exploration Criteria	Very Important	Somewhat Important	Not Important
10. Community Environment (setting where college is located)			
a. Large city (population of 500,000+)	_____	_____	_____
b. Medium city (population 100,000 to 499,000)	_____	_____	_____
c. Small city (population under 100,000)	_____	_____	_____
d. Suburban setting near major urban center	_____	_____	_____
e. Small town	_____	_____	_____
f. Rural community	_____	_____	_____
g. International city	_____	_____	_____
_____	_____	_____	_____
11. Campus and Community Environment			
a. Student spirit and sense of community	_____	_____	_____
b. Friendliness and "feel"	_____	_____	_____
c. Student–faculty relationships	_____	_____	_____
d. Diverse student population	_____	_____	_____
e. Cultural climate	_____	_____	_____
f. Social atmosphere/climate	_____	_____	_____
g. Security	_____	_____	_____
h. Faith-based needs and interests	_____	_____	_____
i. Opportunity to participate in the following sport(s):	_____	_____	_____
_____	_____	_____	_____
_____	_____	_____	_____
j. Opportunity to participate in the following extracurricular activities:	_____	_____	_____
_____	_____	_____	_____
_____	_____	_____	_____

Exploration Criteria	Very Important	Somewhat Important	Not Important
k. Comfortable dormitories	_____	_____	_____
l. Healthy and appealing food services	_____	_____	_____
m. Comfortable off-campus housing (when and if required)	_____	_____	_____
n. Accessible campus (easy to move about)	_____	_____	_____
o. Attractive campus and facilities	_____	_____	_____
p. Recreational and leisure time activities	_____	_____	_____
q. Weekend/social/entertainment opportunities	_____	_____	_____
r. Opportunity to participate in campus or community religious activities	_____	_____	_____
s. Health and/or physical facilities	_____	_____	_____
t. _____	_____	_____	_____
u. _____	_____	_____	_____
v. _____	_____	_____	_____

12. College Costs and Student Assistance

	Very Important	Somewhat Important	Not Important
a. Cost of tuition, room and board, and related costs and fees	_____	_____	_____
b. Availability of grants and scholarships	_____	_____	_____
c. Availability of loans	_____	_____	_____
d. Opportunities for part-time work on campus	_____	_____	_____
e. Opportunities for part-time work in community	_____	_____	_____
f. _____	_____	_____	_____
g. _____	_____	_____	_____

CHAPTER 6

High School Course Selection: Relevance to College Admission

If there is a single factor that will influence your getting into the college of your choice, it will likely be your record of academic achievement and the quality of the courses in which that achievement was earned. Survey after survey of college admission officers by the National Association for College Admission Counseling (NACAC) point to a strong academic record in a challenging program of studies as the applicant's strongest ally in the college admission process.

All during high school you have been or will be given the opportunity to select or elect courses. This is a point of empowerment in your education, a time when your immediate action can have a significant influence on events in the distant future.

Throughout the high school experience you should design a challenging curricular experience, one where you are able to address the challenges and graduate with a strong academic record, as reflected in your final grade point average (GPA). In a competitive admission environment, the strength of your academic record could tip the admission scales in your favor. College admission officers know the difference between an advanced level mathematics course and one that requires less study and personal attention.

There are no guarantees or so-called locks in the college admission process—even class valedictorians and students with seemingly invincible GPAs are routinely turned down by some highly competitive institutions. It means these colleges are looking for students who have a certain mix of academic and personal characteristics, elements they specifically desire in incoming students. In these situations, criteria other than a strong academic record in a challenging curriculum are influencing the admission formula.

As a rule, competitive or selective colleges want to admit students who have experienced success in a rigorous academic environment and appear capable of continuing that success at the collegiate level. The courses listed here are typical of a strong college preparatory schedule:

- English (four years)
- Science (three to four years, including biology, chemistry, physics, and/or earth science)
- Mathematics (three to four years, including algebra I and II, geometry, trigonometry, and/or calculus)
- History/Social Studies (three to four years)
- Foreign Language (three to four years of the same language)
- Computer Science
- Art and Music

Anyone whose academic abilities allow him or her to participate in Advanced Placement or International Baccalaureate level classes should always do so; those reviewing the admission application will undoubtedly view taking such courses positively. With respect to academic record and individual achievement, you should not minimize the importance of courses taken in the senior year—if for no other reason than for the maintenance of a strong work ethic. This is not a time to reduce one's load or cut back on effort.

Consider your education like the conditioning associated with an athletic endeavor. Once a peak level of performance is achieved, you must go into a "maintenance" mode. Otherwise, you will fall out of shape and not be able to sustain the same level of achievement. The so-called senior slump represents a break in conditioning and could result in unnecessary difficulty in college, and, in extreme cases, may even result in the reversal of a previously favorable admission decision.

Think of the college admission formula as a recipe. Most institutions factor the same ingredients into their admission decisions—academic achievement, test scores, teacher or counselor recommendations, and so forth. But, as is often the case with culinary recipes, the chef (in this instance, the college) may rely a bit more or a bit less on a particular ingredient. The main ingredient in most college admission recipes, however, is the level of student performance in a strong curriculum. Translated into simple terms: "study challenging subjects and achieve the best grades possible."

Student Exercise 6.1

TRACKING YOUR HIGH SCHOOL STUDIES

In the space provided below, list the college preparatory courses that you have completed (or plan to complete), freshman through senior year:

Freshman Year or earlier   **Grade**

_____

_____

_____

_____

_____

_____

Sophomore Year   **Grade**

_____

_____

_____

_____

_____

Junior Year   **Grade**

_____

_____

_____

_____

_____

Senior Year   **Grade**

_____

_____

_____

_____

_____

_____

Summer Study   **Grade**

_____

_____

College Level Courses Taken before College

_____

_____

_____

Note: If you cannot remember course titles or sequences, your counselor or school registrar can help you complete the above information.

CHAPTER 7

Learning about College Options: Getting the Best Information

When it comes to gathering information about colleges, students will find an incredible array of sources. Approach the reference shelf in your local library or the college and career resource center at your high school and you'll find a number of well-used publications that have been placed there to help you. These materials will aid in your general study of colleges and answer the specific questions that you have about particular institutions and their programs. In these times of high-tech communication, videos, computers, and online systems are also used to get college information to the prospective student.

Using College and Education Information

As you acquire information about colleges, be sure to consider these factors as you evaluate your sources:

- Accuracy—Colleges are changing, dynamic places and you will want to make certain that you're using the latest edition of any publication or information source.
- Variety—Be certain to use a variety of information sources. Some are great for general information; others are better at presenting details. Multiple sources also allow you to perform accuracy cross-checks.
- Information overload— Spread out your exploration activities so that you can consume all that you are learning. Too much information acquired too quickly can lead to confusion and frustration. Enjoy the college exploration venture.

Sources of College and Educational Information

Use the following information sources in your personal search:

- Guidance publications—Spend a little time at the beginning of the search examining the general guides. These resources will help you form questions and structure your college exploration.
- College guides/directories—These are the big, telephone book look-alikes and are produced by publishers such as Peterson's, Barron's, and the College Board. They contain a page or a column on two thousand or more colleges and are great for fact-finding (e.g., college costs, majors, size), but don't judge a college solely by what's in these publications.
- Viewbooks and catalogs—Generated by individual colleges, these publications provide in-depth information about admission criteria, programs of study, student life, and much more.
- Internet websites—Every college has a website to disseminate admission and financial aid information and communicate with prospective students. Students can access these websites by visiting general Internet search engines like Google, America Online, or Yahoo! and inserting the name of the college after the keyword inquiry. Most colleges allow students to complete their application online and either submit it electronically or print out and mail it. Other institutions have created virtual college tours, chat rooms, and electronic newsletters. A growing number are offering webinars and other Internet programs to exchange information with prospective students. Website-driven information has the advantage of being the most current available.
- Videos and webcasts—Produced by colleges, these programs afford students an opportunity to take a tour of the campus and check in on a variety of campus activities without ever having to leave home.
- Computerized guidance information systems—School-based interactive systems permit students to conduct their college search by matching their needs and interests with the offerings of particular colleges.

All of these resources can provide good information that will contribute to quality exploration and sound decision making. They should not, however, be the only sources.

Students can personalize their information quest when they interact with the college admission counselors who visit high schools and participate in local college fair programs. Seize every opportunity to interface with reliable sources.

Finally, as you refine choices, campus visits become a "must" on your exploration agenda. College visits are a reality check of sorts: your firsthand opportunity to see and feel the college . . . to try it on for a "fit." Don't miss it!

Frequently Asked Questions

Question: When should I send away for college viewbooks, brochures, and applications?

Answer: There really isn't a precise time to begin collecting information about colleges. It will vary from student to student. Start early enough to allow for a thorough search. A good time to become actively engaged in information collection is any time during the junior year. Any earlier and you take the risk that significant information will change before you apply and enroll.

If you take the ACT or SAT examination, you can indicate on the test form that you want your name and address made available to colleges that will send you literature. Information can also be collected at college fairnight programs where you can also interact with admission representatives. While most information contained in college publications remains current, some things (e.g., costs, deadline dates) may change or vary from year to year. When it comes time to apply to college, make sure you have the current college application and follow the most recent application procedures and submission dates.

Question: Are some college guidance tools or resources better than others?

Answer: You have probably discovered what other college-bound students have: there are many guides, directories, computer disks, and videos purporting to be the best at helping guide you through the college exploration and application process. Several pieces of advice are appropriate here. First, look to the tried and tested college guides and tools, the ones that have been around a few years. Their mere survival attests to their usefulness and quality. Second, ask your counselor or librarian what resources they recommend. Finally, remember to visit colleges and talk with admission representatives. They will complement the information you retrieve from the guides and related tools.

Question: There are a number of college videos and DVDs in my school's college and career center. Can I learn much by watching them?

Answer: College videos and DVDs crashed onto the scene in the 1980s and have been around ever since. Most present an accurate and balanced look at the school, offering a visual and audio alternative to all the print resources. Others, however, can be extremely biased, presenting only the parts of the college they want you to see. Counselors have been concerned about the shortage of classroom and instructional scenes as opposed to what appears to be an overload of campus life and social depiction. College videos, taken in context as one of many sources of information, can help you examine your options. Don't make your final decision based solely on what you see and hear on the video. In addition to the videotapes and DVDs, which you can borrow from your school's college and career center or library, many colleges now have their admission presentation online or will send you a personal copy to view.

Question: How can I make sense of all the college information I receive?

Answer: If you're receiving a large volume of college literature, you'll want to create a system to keep the information organized. Consider designing a chart that indicates "Name of College," "Date Information Received," and a "Notes" section that will help you evaluate the school. If you haven't received information from a school you want to consider, make a note and contact the school again. Based on your review, start to prioritize your materials, putting the more popular options on the top of the pile. Once you've begun your preliminary exploration, discard the information about colleges you're no longer considering.

Question: How can I make the most of a special college program at my high school?

Answer: Programs for college-bound students at the high school afford you and your parents the unique opportunity of meeting with a number of admission representatives at a single event and getting answers to the questions that are important to you. Like the "prepping" you will do before the larger college fairs, some advance work is in order. Begin by obtaining a list of participating colleges from your counselor. Then review their viewbooks and application materials to see what questions these materials might generate. Finally, make a list of the general topics and questions you want to address at the event. Do this homework and you're certain to impress the admission representative.

Question: Why don't more admission representatives visit my high school?

Answer: Colleges assign their admission counselors to visit high schools according to varying philosophies. Many make certain to visit the schools that traditionally send them students. Others attempt to visit all of the high schools in what they consider to be the area (region or state) where they are best known and are most likely to draw student applications. Still others seek to recruit from a much larger map and will send admission representatives almost anywhere in the nation. However, when the map gets this big, they are not always able to make annual visits. Finally, colleges have been hit by budget restrictions in recent years, and recruiting activities, especially the long-distance trips, have been included in the items being cut or contained.

Question: How useful will college guides be in my search?

Answer: College guides, the big telephone book look-alikes, have been a staple in the college exploration literature for a very long time. Each contains a page or a column on a particular college and are great for finding details about costs, location, majors, size, and so on: the kind of information students need to acquire early on in the exploration process. The best guides update their information annually and it is crucial that you work with the most current edition. Like other sources of college admission and financial aid information, you should not judge any college solely by what's in any single publication. However, when considered with other sources and a visit, this information can be very valuable.

Student Exercise 7.1

FINDING AND USING COLLEGE GUIDANCE RESOURCES

In the space below, keep track of the various publications, computer disks, video or DVD programs, and related guidance resources that you use during the college exploration and decision-making process. Be certain to identify where you found the resource (e.g., library, guidance office, college and career center) in case you wish to use it later in the process.

Resource Title   Location   Comments

Example:

Peterson's Guide to   Good reference to general
Four Year Colleges   School library   information about colleges

_____

_____

_____

_____

_____

_____

_____

_____

_____

_____

_____

_____

_____

_____

_____

_____

Student Exercise 7.2

HUMAN INFORMATION SOURCES: PREPARING TO MEET COLLEGE ADMISSION REPRESENTATIVES

In the space provided below, make a list of colleges and universities that you expect to be visiting your school or participating in future college fair programs. Following each institution, write in the specific questions you wish to ask the admission representative(s).

College: _____

Questions:

_____

_____

_____

College: _____

Questions:

_____

_____

_____

College: _____

Questions:

_____

_____

_____

College: _____

Questions:

_____

_____

_____

General questions for representatives of all college fair programs:

_____

_____

_____

CHAPTER 8

Using the Internet to Explore and Apply to Colleges

In the span of a few years, the Internet has become a valuable and reliable source of information about colleges and a trusted mechanism for making application for admission and financial aid online. Every two- and four-year college in the United States has a website.

At these websites students can obtain information about programs of study, admission requirements, college costs, and frequently asked questions (FAQs) that will guide them in making their college decisions. Students with access to a personal computer with an Internet hookup at home or in their school or library should take advantage of this information vehicle and use it throughout the exploration and application process.

While Internet websites will vary remarkably in the breadth of information they offer and their user friendliness, they are usually reliable with respect to both the accuracy and timeliness of the information that is posted there. Prospective students must remember these are public information sites where a college wishes to put forward a positive view of itself. Information gathered from websites, like print and other information, must be evaluated.

Students can access individual college websites often by typing "www."—followed by the name—followed by "edu." Example: www.dickinson.edu will take you directly to Dickinson College's website. Often it is a variation or twist on the name—Shippensburg University's website, for example, can be found at www.ship.edu. Should you fail to access the website by the college name, the next best route is to go through one of the major search engines like www.google.com or www.yahoo.com and use either their education directory or the college name to get you to the institution you wish to explore.

Most college websites offer you a link to the admission or financial aid pages, and here again, they vary in both usability and content. Some offer just the basics; others are very sophisticated—like allowing you to take a virtual tour of their campus, including both visual and audio messages.

In addition to institution websites, there are a number of general Internet locations where students can obtain information and conduct searches of college databases. The U.S. Department of Education's aboutcollege (www.college.gov) and College Navigator websites (nces.ed.gov/collegenavigator) are excellent Internet resources. Others can be found at www.collegeboard.com, www.actstudent.org/college/choosing.html, and www.petersons.com. Most of these Internet sites will allow students to submit search criteria (major field of study, size, location) and narrow their results.

NACAC has created *An Internet Road Map for College-Bound Students*, an innovative, "how to do it" guide to using the Internet in the college admission process. The resource can be found online at: www.nacacnet.org/MemberPortal/News/StepsNewsletter/An+Internet+Road+Map+for+the+College-Bound+Student.htm.

The same is true for general financial aid information. At these Internet sites, students can conduct scholarship searches, estimate college costs, and determine financial aid eligibility by using their online calculators. Among the best of these sites is www.nasfaa.org, a resource sponsored by the National Association of Student Financial Aid Administrators. Another is www.fastweb.org. You may also wish to visit www.finaid.org or the websites of banks that offer student loans.

Once a prospective student has determined the colleges to which he or she wishes to apply, the chances are likely that the institution will allow him or her to apply online. Here again, the application features vary. The colleges out in front in the use of information technology will allow their applicants to complete the admission application, pay registration fees, submit essays—all electronically. Most will have variations of these features. Applications for scholarships and financial aid may also be completed and submitted this way.

Finally, students using the Internet to explore and apply can also establish ongoing communication with the colleges that interest them. Many conduct live, interactive webinars, disseminate electronic newsletters, and offer chat rooms for prospective students. They may even hook you up with "e-pals," current students with whom you can exchange e-mail correspondence.

If you have mastered the world of electronic communication, add the Internet to your college exploration and application strategies and let cyberspace be one more ally in your information quest.

Frequently Asked Questions

Question: How successful can I expect to be using the Internet to gather information about colleges?

Answer: A few minutes browsing the Internet can lead to a remarkable discovery. Thousands of American colleges and universities have placed admission and financial aid information on their home pages and each is finding new and innovative ways of using technology to tell their story and communicate with prospective students.

In some instances, these websites are restricted to visual and text presentations, the same information that is currently contained in viewbooks. Others, however, have added the interactive features that allow you to request personal information and interact personally with a member of the admission staff. The Internet has created a unique capability for colleges and universities to place comprehensive admission information at your fingertips.

Student Exercise 8.1

INTERNET SITES THAT HELP WITH COLLEGE EXPLORATION AND APPLICATION

Create and maintain a list of your favorite college admission and financial aid websites and the Internet locations you will want to keep for future reference.

General college exploration and admission websites:

_____   _____

_____   _____

Scholarship and financial aid websites:

_____   _____

_____   _____

Specific college and university websites:

_____   _____

_____   _____

CHAPTER 9

Making the Most of the College Fair Experience

During your high school years, you will most likely have an opportunity to participate in a college fair, an event where representatives from a number of colleges and universities gather in one place to meet prospective students and present information about their institutions and programs. Interaction with college representatives allows you to get answers to your personal questions and clarify or correct information that you acquired from other sources.

College fairs come in various sizes and formats. Small events of ten to thirty colleges may be held at your school. Larger fairs are often sponsored by a school district or group of schools and are held in a central location. The biggest fairs, attracting hundreds of colleges, are those sponsored by the National Association for College Admission Counseling (NACAC). The NACAC fairs are typically held in large civic centers and are attended by students from a large city or metropolitan area. Participate in more than one fair if they are available to you.

College fairs provide you with a unique opportunity to talk directly with admission officers or counselors or with alumni or student representatives who assist the college in its admission efforts. A bit of preparation on your part will allow you to gain more from the experience than if you simply walk into the fair "cold."

1. Do your college fair homework. Study the list of participating colleges (if available) and prepare a list of questions. Review their literature and visit their website in advance of the fair. Take your questions to the fair and don't be shy about asking them.
2. Be prepared to complete many student inquiry cards. To expedite this process, you can prepare preaddressed labels that can be affixed to the college's card or cards with your name and contact information. You may wish to jot

down your area of academic interest and any desired information (e.g., view-book or application request, scholarship criteria, etc.) on the card you leave with the representative.

3. Allow sufficient time to talk with as many college representatives as possible. If you are undecided about where to apply, use the fair to continue your exploration. While many colleges will be familiar to you, others will not. If you have narrowed your list of colleges, the fair will permit you to be more focused in your information quest, but you may wish to engage in discussion with some colleges that are not currently on your consideration list. Be open to new information and interface with colleges that are new to you. It's part of the discovery process.

4. Allow time to attend the admission and financial aid seminars that may be offered as part of the fair program. Presented by experts in the field, these seminars offer valuable guidance to aid you in the decision-making and application processes.

5. Bring pencils, paper, or a notebook and take time to jot down the answers to your questions and other information that you deem important. Carry a shoulder bag or knapsack as many of the colleges will have information that they wish to leave with you.

6. Note the name of the admission representative with whom you spoke and take some time after the fair to write follow-up notes or letters to those colleges for which you have special questions. Targeted letters get faster responses than the "to whom it may concern" variety.

7. Talk with your fellow students after the fair and compare notes regarding the information you received and the impressions that were created. Comparing your insights and experiences with others may generate perspectives that were not apparent before. Your counselor can also help you to digest all of the information you have acquired.

8. Present yourself in the best possible manner. The college fair is an opportunity for you to interact face-to-face with college admission representatives, individuals who might eventually be involved in reviewing your application and contributing to the admission decision. Make a powerful first impression with this individual. Just like you jotted down a few points on your inquiry card, the admission representative may have made a few notes about you after you walked away.

Note: When preparing for college fairs, complete Student Exercise 7.2, Human Information Sources: Preparing to Meet College Admission Representatives. This information will help you navigate the college fair to your greatest advantage.

Frequently Asked Questions

Question: How can I determine where the major college fairs in the nation will be held?

Answer: The largest network of national college fairs are those sponsored by the National Association for College Admission Counseling. They've been doing fairs for a quarter century and put on the very best programs. NACAC sponsors fairs in more than thirty American cities each year. To get a list of NACAC fair locations, dates, and times, go to: www.nacacnet.org/MemberPortal/Events/CollegeFairs. NACAC also sponsors a series of fairs that provide information to students about the performing arts.

CHAPTER 10

Campus Visits: Getting Ready to Go

Choosing a college is more than choosing a place to study and learn. You are also selecting the home where you will live during the next two, four, or maybe more years. Some admission officers express concern that as many as one-fourth of their freshmen students do not step foot on campus until they have arrived to start classes. This lack of hands-on investigation may contribute to the dismal retention statistics at some colleges.

To this point your exploration has probably been concentrated on the information that you have been able to gather from guidance resources, your visits to college websites, and from interaction with people. As the list gets smaller and your exploration becomes more refined, the remaining colleges merit the scrutiny of a campus visit.

Whether your campus visit will be productive may depend on the tasks that you complete in advance of your departure date. Consider the following:

1. Let the admission office know that you're coming. This notice will allow you to visit a class or two, participate in a guided tour, take part in an admission interview (if required) and meet with representatives of the financial aid office. By planning ahead, you may also have an opportunity to stay overnight in a dormitory. If you arrive without notice, these options may not be available to you.
2. If you have friends or know alumni from your high school attending the college, arrange to visit with them during your visit. Your counselor may be able to identify some students for you to contact.
3. When trying to determine the best time for a college visit, there are a number of factors to consider. To get the true feel of a college, it is best to visit while it is in session and, therefore, alive with activity. Ideally, you will have refined your choices and be prepared to conduct some visits during the spring of your junior year. If not, set aside some time early in your senior year.

4. Some colleges hold open houses or special admission-orientation programs. There are pluses and minuses associated with these events, and you will need to determine if what you are trying to find out about the college will be served by your participation. The major negative with formal orientation programs is that you and your fellow visitors get a canned presentation, some of which will test your ability to sit still and listen.

5. Arrange a schedule that allows parent or guardian participation. Colleges welcome parental involvement and often will provide special activities for them.

6. Create an itinerary that allows you to visit more than one campus on the same trip. The *Rand McNally Road Atlas*, which lists American colleges, is an excellent tool for trip planning. If you are traveling long distances, ask the admission office if they have arrangements with airlines for discounted student travel fares. Take advantage of seasonal and special airfares. The Amtrak system has a discount ticket price for students and parents who want to visit colleges via rail.

7. Make certain that your schedule affords you not only ample opportunity to visit the college, but also time to check out the community in which the college is located. Even if you love the college, you don't want to become a campus "prisoner" or be required to exit on weekends to have a reasonable social, recreational, or cultural life.

8. Prepare for the visit by making a checklist of the specific things you want to view and by creating a list of questions you wish to ask. Take your camera along to shoot some informal shots of the surroundings to serve as a reminder of the visit.

Remember, you wouldn't buy a jacket or pair of shoes without trying them on first or a car without a test drive. Don't commit to your collegiate experience without a similar trial. This is your chance to play detective and get the answers to all of your important questions. Use the campus visit approach that you are trying on each college to see "how it fits." It may save you from a day when you look back and say, "I wish I would have known."

Note: Just like your preparation for college fairs, you need to get ready to go on your campus visit with your homework done and your questions ready. Along with Student Exercise 10.1, which follows, you may also want to revisit Student Exercise 7.2, Human Information Sources: Preparing to Meet College Admission Representatives. The information generated by these two exercises will help you make the most of each campus visit.

Frequently Asked Questions

Question: How can I get a behind-the-scenes look at the colleges I'm interested in, not just the standard tour the admission office wants me to experience?

Answer: You have several options. First, allow yourself sufficient time to visit both the campus and the community beyond that which you get to see on the official tour. Consider connecting with someone on campus who is capable of giving you the insider tour, possibly a friend or recent graduate from your high school who is currently enrolled at the college. If you feel that the admission tour didn't allow sufficient time for examination of any portion of the campus, return to these spots for a second and more thorough examination.

Question: I am planning to visit colleges in the near future. How important is it to sit in on a class?

Answer: Very important. Although you will probably need to get prior approval from the instructor, you shouldn't pass up the opportunity to sit in on a few classes. You'll get a feel for the academic challenge, teaching methods, and level of student participation. Try to stick around after class and talk with the professor and the students. They can answer your questions and tell you if the class is typical of the college.

Question: What should I do if time or expense prohibits me from visiting a distant campus before I make my decision to apply?

Answer: This happens more than you would expect. Make a concerted effort to get as much information as you can about the college and be certain that it meets what you're looking for in a college from an academic perspective. Also examine descriptive and demographic information to ensure that it has the things you want to study, is the right size, and meets the other criteria you deem important. It would help to talk with recent graduates or persons you know who also know the college.

If you are admitted before seeing the college, make every attempt to visit before you enroll. Otherwise, college will be somewhat like a blind date. Some are great, others not so great!

Question: Should I spend an overnight on campus and, if so, what should I look for?

Answer: An overnight stay will extend the time you have to evaluate the college and determine if it possesses what you are looking for. Many colleges now provide accommodations (housing and meals) for prospective students and their parents. This extra time will also allow you to see the college after hours, during which you might also attend a campus event or spend some time talking with current students. Overnight stays can be very time-consuming if you're attempting to visit multiple campuses, but the time may be well spent.

Student Exercise 10.1

PREPARING FOR THE COLLEGE VISIT

In order for campus visits to be constructive and a valuable use of your time, it is necessary for you to engage in some pre-visit planning. Develop an itinerary and make the necessary contacts to ensure that you see the things you wish to see and get answers to your questions.

College _____

Contact person: _____ Telephone # _____

Date of visit: _____ Time: _____

Official admission interview: _____ Yes _____ No

People you wish to visit:

Name	Telephone #	Appointment time	Location
_____	_____	_____	_____
_____	_____	_____	_____
_____	_____	_____	_____
_____	_____	_____	_____

Questions for admission representatives:

_____

_____

_____

_____

_____

Questions for students on campus:

_____

_____

_____

_____

_____

Questions for faculty members:

_____

_____

_____

_____

_____

Things you want to see on campus:

_____

_____

_____

_____

_____

Things you want to see in college community:

_____

_____

_____

_____

_____

Note: Make a similar list for each college visit.

CHAPTER 11

Campus Visits: Being There and Afterward

You've arrived on campus. It's bigger than you thought it would be. No, it's smaller. Which buildings are the dorms? Which are the classrooms? There is a buzz of excitement about the campus. It's rather sedate. The students appear friendly. All, some, or none of these impressions may greet you when you make your campus visits, but each contributes to the personality of the college; a personality that you should try to define while you are there.

The mission of your campus visit is twofold. First, you want to get answers to the specific and general questions that you have determined are important to you in your college selection. In some instances, you will be looking for reaffirmation of information that you have acquired from other sources. Second, you are conducting a test or trial of sorts. This up close and personal view of the college—limited as it may be—will allow you to get the feel of the place—to "try it on for fit."

During each visit to a campus, you should attempt to have as many of the following experiences as possible. Otherwise, a return visit may be warranted.

1. Sit in on a class or two. If possible, find a class whose subject is of interest to you. While the time will be very short, you can assess the level of student enthusiasm, the degree to which they seem prepared, and some sense of teaching styles.
2. Talk with a professor, department chair, or academic advisor. Ask about the academic requirements, program of studies, class size, instructional strategies, and other academic matters. Inform them of your academic experiences in high school and collegiate goals and invite their appraisal or comment.
3. Check out the library, computer, and science labs and other learning support facilities. If you have particular learning needs, talk with those providing that assistance or service.

4. Examine the total living environment, including the dormitories, dining halls, recreational facilities, student center—all of the places where you will spend time when not in the classroom. Are these facilities clean, comfortable, and attractive? Do the facilities offer privacy when desired? Sample the food and determine if your dietary needs and preferences can be met. Are there places to relax, play, and enjoy some "down time?"

5. Talk with students. Let them know that you're considering applying. Do they seem friendly, enthusiastic, and responsive to your questions? Ask what they would have liked to have known before enrolling, but didn't.

6. Participate in a guided tour. Listen to the guide's presentation and ask questions that it may generate. Take your own informal tour. Go back to those places that aroused your curiosity or where you didn't get to spend enough time. Wander away from the campus to see what the community surrounding the college is like.

7. If the college requires a personal interview as part of the admission process, schedule this activity while you're on campus. Prepare for the interview, including making a list of questions you wish to ask. If you're interested in the college, let that interest show!

8. Keep your eyes and ears open. What is the general physical condition of the college? Is the campus atmosphere to your liking? Are there lines and crowds? How do students dress? Bulletin boards and posters tell many stories about campus life or the lack thereof. Take notes. Pick up things (e.g., student newspapers) along the way. Take some pictures. Jot down a few notes right after the visit while information and impressions are fresh and clear. Use all of your senses!

9. Send thank you notes to any hosts or individuals that took time to help you and answer your questions.

CSI is a very popular television series and you are about to be engaged in a personal CSI of sorts, your college scene investigation. Look for every clue. Let no corner of the campus escape your study. Question all the "witnesses." Very soon you will be refining your list of prospective colleges even more. Each campus visit will contribute to the two decisions you will soon be making: where to apply and where to enroll if admitted.

Frequently Asked Questions

Question: If an interview is not a part of the college visit itinerary, should I ask for one?

Answer: There are several conditions under which you might wish to request an interview. One, if there is any aspect of your educational experience (e.g., death in the family or health problems that affected your academic performance) that can't be conveyed via the application or require detailed explanation, you might want to use a personal interview with an admission officer or counselor to present that information. Second, if you have personal questions that you don't want to ask a college tour guide or feel comfortable asking in a group forum, you can request an interview to acquire this information. Basically, you should use any optional strategy whenever you need additional information or think it will strengthen your application.

Student Exercise 11.1

CAMPUS VISIT REPORT FORM: EXPERIENCES AND IMPRESSIONS

Following each campus visit take a few minutes to write down your impressions and evaluate the experience. Also jot down any remaining questions or concerns that need to be addressed if you are to keep this college on your prospect list. After you have completed all of your college visits, put the report forms side by side and compare the information contained on each.

College: _____ Date visited: _____

Check each of the activities you experienced and places you visited:

_____ Campus tour (guided)   _____ Library
_____ Campus tour (on your own)   _____ Computer, science, and related labs
_____ Class observation(s)   _____ Recreational facilities
_____ Student interview(s)   _____ Athletic event
_____ Professor interview(s)   _____ Concert, play, or cultural event
_____ Admission officer interview   _____ Campus store
_____ Financial aid officer interview _____ Community tour
_____ Dormitory   Other, specify below:
_____ Dining hall   _____ _____
_____ Student union/campus center   _____ _____

Special Experiences—Did you experience any of the following?

Observe a college class or classes: _____ Yes _____ No If yes, what were your impressions?

_____

_____

_____

_____

Meet with professors or other staff members: _____ Yes _____ No If yes, what were your impressions?

_____

_____

_____

Meet with students: _____ Yes _____ No If yes, what were your impressions?

_____

_____

_____

_____

_____

Stay overnight in a dorm: _____ Yes _____ No If yes, what were your impressions?

_____

_____

_____

_____

_____

Read the college newspaper or examine the items posted on the student union bulletin board: _____ Yes _____ No If yes, what were your impressions?

_____

_____

_____

_____

_____

Take a walk or ride around the community in which the college is located: _____ Yes _____ No If yes, what were your impressions?

_____

_____

_____

_____

_____

Note: Make additional copies of this report form for each college visit.

Student Exercise 11.2

EVALUATING THE COLLEGE VISIT

Rate your impression of the following academic, student life, and related elements as experienced or observed during your campus visit. Circle the number that best reflects your impression. If other features influenced you favorably or unfavorably, list the items in one of the vacant spaces and rate it accordingly.

College _____   Rating

	Favorable			Unfavorable	
Academic climate and competition	5	4	3	2	1
Student spirit and enthusiasm	5	4	3	2	1
Friendliness and geniality	5	4	3	2	1
Class size	5	4	3	2	1
Instructional style	5	4	3	2	1
Instructional facilities/classrooms	5	4	3	2	1
Library, laboratories, and support facilities	5	4	3	2	1
Living and social facilities					
Dorms	5	4	3	2	1
Dining hall	5	4	3	2	1
Student union/center	5	4	3	2	1
Size of college	5	4	3	2	1
Student composition and diversity	5	4	3	2	1
Location of the college	5	4	3	2	1
Campus atmosphere and environment	5	4	3	2	1
Church, cultural, and related opportunities	5	4	3	2	1
Fitness facilities (gym/pool/running trails)	5	4	3	2	1
Community environment	5	4	3	2	1
Social life/extracurricular activities	5	4	3	2	1
_____	5	4	3	2	1
_____	5	4	3	2	1
_____	5	4	3	2	1

General observations:

_____

_____

_____

_____

Note: Make additional copies of this report form for each college visit.

CHAPTER 12

Admission Plans: Modes of Admission Access

When the time arrives to apply to a college or university, the student will find that institutions offer a number of plans for the submission of applications. Depending where you are in your personal exploration and decision making, one of these plans may suit your particular application requirements. Review and consider all admission plan options. Consult with your school counselor or the admission counselor at the specific college if you have any concerns or questions.

Regular Decision

The majority of college-bound students will submit their application by a specified date and receive a decision in a clearly defined period of time or by a formally acknowledged date. This is known as the regular decision plan and students can file as many applications under the plan as they wish. Upon acceptance, students have until May 1 to confirm their intention to enroll.

Rolling Admission

The colleges and universities that review student applications as they are received and render almost immediate admission decisions use what is called a rolling admission plan. Institutions that receive a large number of applications use this approach simply to manage the volume of application activity. Student notification of the admission decision can usually be expected in three to four weeks following receipt of the application.

Students that apply to a college under a rolling admission plan can apply to other colleges and consider all offers of admission and financial aid (by May 1) before being required to declare their intention to enroll or file the required admission and housing deposits.

Early Action

Under the early action plan, the student applies early and learns of the college's acceptance or rejection well in advance of the regular cycle and response date. Students are not restricted from applying to other institutions and have until May 1 to consider their options and confirm enrollment.

Early Decision

This plan was created to help the capable, informed, and committed student apply to the institution that she or he has identified as a first choice. For students who have engaged in quality exploration and arrived at a sound decision, this is an excellent plan. Under the early decision plan the student makes a binding commitment to his or her first-choice institution, where, if admitted, the student pledges to enroll. It has the benefit of bringing closure to one's personal application activity early in the senior year while others are still completing forms.

Restricted Early Action

This plan allows the student to apply to an institution of preference and receive an early admission decision. They may, however, be restricted from applying through early decision, early action, or restricted early action to other institutions, a condition that will be explained by the application procedures of the college or colleges. If offered enrollment, the student has until May 1 to confirm.

Universal Reply Date

Most colleges adhere to the universal reply date of May 1 as the deadline given to students to consider offers of admission and declare their enrollment intention. Students, however, may feel pressure to commit earlier. If this happens, you should contact the appropriate admission or financial aid counselor to explain your circumstances and where you are in the decision-making process. Most will honor the May 1 date.

Frequently Asked Questions

Question: What are the circumstances under which an "early" application might be appropriate?

Answer: Early action, early decision, and restricted early action plans were created to help the informed and committed student who is ready to apply and they allow the applicant to bring closure to the application process earlier in the senior year. On the negative side, early plans are not the best direction to take if the student has a high level of financial need and requires additional time to negotiate an attractive financial aid package. In these instances, it may be wise to apply to multiple colleges and compare financial aid offers. Finally, don't apply early just to be done with the process or because you hear it is the best way to get in. It has to be right for you. Your counselor and the admission representative at the college can provide information about the nuances of any particular early plan.

CHAPTER 13

Degree of Difficulty: Understanding the Admission Competition

Will I be accepted? That's the question that you have probably asked yourself a hundred times as you look at colleges and consider applying for admission. According to an annual study conducted by the Higher Education Research Institute at UCLA, more than 90 percent of college freshmen surveyed said they were attending their first or second choice college. This is the result of good exploration and decision making.

As you refine your options and move in the direction of making application, you need to evaluate your prospects of acceptance at the college or colleges that you have determined are right for you. When it comes to the consideration of your application, colleges fall into one of several competitive categories. Understanding these categories will help you to file applications that improve your chances of being admitted.

College Categories

SELECTIVE COLLEGES

The great majority of colleges and universities are selective, meaning that they require students to meet specific selection criteria in order to be considered for admission. The rigor will vary, but students that match or exceed the criteria stand the best chance of admission.

COMPETITIVE COLLEGES

When more students apply than the college can accommodate, the result is heightened competition for limited space. The more applications filed with an institution—the more competitive it will be to gain admission. There are many stories about Ivy League colleges that reject the applications of dozens of valedictorians each year. You probably know some very capable students who weren't admitted to highly competitive colleges. If you're a valid candidate for admission to such colleges, you should consider filing three or four applications to increase your chances of admission to one of them.

OPEN ADMISSION COLLEGES

"Open" admission colleges, like community colleges and technical institutes, invite applications from interested students possessing a high school diploma or its equivalent and admit most of the students that apply. Admission to specific programs (e.g., nursing, technology, etc.) within these institutions, however, may require more stringent criteria.

Students that successfully complete their high school's college preparatory program are likely to be admissible to many colleges. Remember, even if you are denied admission to a college, you have other avenues to the same goal. Don't be afraid to try to be admitted.

Understanding Institutional Selectivity and Competitiveness

How do you determine the selectivity or competitiveness of the colleges you're exploring? Consider the following:

1. Examine the characteristics of the students the college is currently admitting, the students that you'll be competing with in class each day. This information is contained in the annual freshman class profile—a composite of the academic demographics of the most recently admitted class.
2. Review the application, acceptance, and enrollment statistics of the most recently admitted class. How many applied? How many were accepted? How many actually enrolled. This information is published in many of the general college guidebooks. If you can't find it, ask an admission representative for the statistics.
3. Talk with students and former students of the colleges. They know firsthand what the academic climate is like. Ask counselors, teachers, and admission officers. They've worked with students who have preceded you and enrolled at the same institutions you are considering.

4. Examine the retention statistics. Many college graduates earned their degrees at colleges that they found after they experienced academic difficulty at their first college. The reasons for transferring can vary (e.g., living and social issues, financial, etc.), but you should never invite academic difficulty by trying to gain admission to a college where your prospects for success are not reasonable.

This information, coupled with a realistic assessment of your personal abilities and interests, can point you toward colleges where you are most likely to be accepted and, more important, be successful. Your goal is to find a college or colleges where you have the greatest chance of enjoying academic achievement in a satisfying living environment. Aspire to succeed and don't invite failure by attempting to get into any college where you won't be successful.

Frequently Asked Questions

Question: Exactly what does it mean when a college is described as selective or competitive?

Answer: These terms relate directly to your chances of being admitted to a particular college or how your qualifications compare with other applicants and admitted students. Most colleges and universities require that prospective students meet specific selection criteria. These institutions are known as being "selective." If students meet these criteria, they are likely to be admitted. The term "competitive" is used when there are more qualified candidates than the college can accommodate, resulting in heightened competition for limited spaces. The more applicants denied admission, the greater the competition. If you conduct a realistic assessment of your personal academic abilities and interests in light of what the college is looking for, you can apply to colleges where you are most likely to be accepted.

Question: I have some reservations about my ability to meet the scholastic requirements at one or two of the colleges on my list. How can I determine if I'm academically qualified to do the work?

Answer: Your best bet is to discuss your list of colleges with your counselor and the teachers who know both you and the colleges you're examining. After that, take a look at the academic profile of the most recent freshman class admitted to the college. How do your academic qualifications compare with those of the students with whom you will be competing? Finally, discuss your scholastic record with admission counselors and students at the college. One or more of these sources will help you assess your qualifications and help you decide whether to apply.

Question: What is the best way to gain admission to one of the service academies?

Answer: From the very beginning, you need to understand that the nation's military service academies are among the most selective of the nation's colleges, and not only on the basis of academics. The service academies are looking for a special kind of student, one who is willing to make a career commitment to serve in one of the armed forces following graduation. Applicants must be top-notch students, be physically fit, and possess the qualities of leadership found in a military officer.

Applicants must receive an official nomination to the academy, the majority of which are made by members of Congress for students who reside in their state or congressional district. You can obtain information about other nomination categories from your counselor or the admission office at the academy that you would like to attend.

CHAPTER 14

College Admission Tests: Strategies for Preparation

A student once said that the two most anxiety-provoking acronyms in the English language were SAT and ACT, representing the standardized admission instruments or tests administered respectively by the College Board and ACT. The most commonly utilized tests are the Preliminary SAT/National Merit Scholarship Qualifying Test (PSAT/NMSQT), PLAN (Preliminary ACT), SAT Reasoning, SAT Subject Tests, ACT, and the Test of English as a Foreign Language (TOEFL). Students engaged in the more challenging academic curricula will also need to know about Advanced Placement (AP) and International Baccalaureate (IB) exams associated with these programs.

SAT Reasoning Test and SAT Subject Tests

The SAT Reasoning Test and SAT Subject Tests are standardized admission or entrance tests and represent one of the criteria that many colleges use in making their admission decisions. The SAT Reasoning Test measures your reading, mathematical, and writing skills. The PSAT/NMSQT is the practice test for the SAT.

SAT Subject Tests focus on study or subject areas and are required by a small number of colleges that are highly selective and want to factor these scores into their admission and placement decisions. Each test purportedly measures a student's knowledge and skills in a particular academic subject. Additional information about all of the College Board examinations can be found at www.collegeboard.com.

ACT Assessment

The ACT Assessment measures general achievement and is used interchangeably or in lieu of the SAT and the SAT Subject Tests. This test has been designed to measure the student's general educational development and her or his ability to meet the challenges of the collegiate academic experience. The PLAN is the practice test for the ACT Assessment. Additional information about the ACT exams can be found at www.act.org.

Advanced Placement and International Baccalaureate Examinations

The student who has participated in college-level courses in high school may elect to participate in one or more of the many Advanced Placement (AP) examinations offered by College Board (www.apcentral.collegeboard.com) or the International Baccalaureate (IB) examinations administered by International Baccalaureate Organization (www.ibo.org). Successful scores on these challenging exams can lead to earned college credit or advanced standing in collegiate classes after enrollment.

Role of Admission Testing in Admission Decisions

As stated earlier in this guidebook, admission testing is one of the factors that many colleges and universities will use in determining admission of applicants. The operative words above are "one" and "many." Numerous studies—repeated over time—suggest that academic achievement in a strong curriculum is the most influential of the various admission factors, but even a 4.0 grade point average isn't always a guarantee. Your GPA and test scores, along with a number of other factors (e.g., class rank, essay, recommendations, extracurricular activities, interview, etc.) are mixed together into an institutional admission formula that guides admission officers.

You should also know that a growing number of colleges, even institutions with reputations for being highly competitive in their admissions, have chosen to abandon SAT and ACT test scores as an entrance requirement or make them optional. Your counselor should have a list of those schools or you can visit the National Center for Fair and Open Testing (Fairtest) at www.fairtest.org/optinit.htm

and get a current list of institutions where admission tests are not required or are optional.

Your counselor possesses valuable information about which tests you should take, when it is best to take them, when they should be repeated (if necessary), and the process you must follow to properly register for each examination. Both ACT and College Board set examination dates are months in advance of their administration and you need to schedule your personal participation at a time convenient to you.

The important thing is to give admission tests their appropriate attention. Too much attention may result in rising anxiety that often results in the distortion of the importance of the tests. Too little attention means that you have failed to recognize the role of these standardized tests in the admission process and your responsibilities in preparing for them. Aim for balance.

Getting Ready for the Examination

Can you prepare? Do test prep courses work? Are test prep guides and computer software programs useful? How much will my scores improve? The following tips will guide you in your test-preparation and test-taking experiences:

1. Pursue the most challenging studies possible all during the high school experience. A prophetic counselor once stated that you can't cram into eleven weeks what you should have learned in eleven years of school.
2. Read as much as you can. Whether study related or just for fun, reading is a habit that will pay dividends on test day.
3. Participate in extracurricular activities that are an extension of the classroom experience, such as activities that will enhance your language and mathematics knowledge and skills.
4. Acquire and review old editions of the actual admission tests. Many experts believe that your best preparation lies in becoming comfortable as a test taker and familiar with the instruments. What better experience than to take a number of old tests? Your counselor or librarian can help you locate the old ones.
5. If your scores aren't where you'd like them to be, consider taking the test again or taking the other test (SAT to ACT and vice versa). Talk with your counselor about retesting.
6. For some students, a test prep course may be in order. These tutoring sessions are available from your school and/or commercial test prep firms. You may also wish to use the test prep manuals, videos, and computer software materials that have been created to improve scores. Before enrolling in a test prep

class or acquiring these tools, seek the recommendation of your counselor or students who have used the materials. The bottom line is not to expect miracles, and don't fall for outrageous claims of score escalation.

As the formal test date approaches, relax and take the experience in stride. Get plenty of rest before the test and carry some nourishment with you on test day to consume during the scheduled breaks. Admission testing is an important event, but it's not the "life and death" experience that some build it up to be.

Test scores alone won't get you in or keep you out of the vast majority of colleges. Good scores will only enhance your prospects for admission if the other criteria have been met. Low scores may cause the admission officer to look for an explanation or deeper into the other admission requirements.

Frequently Asked Questions

Question: Which will count more—my high school grades or my admission test scores?

Answer: Every college has its own formula for making admission decisions and most will tell you that achievement in college preparatory studies will weigh more heavily in their decision. This is supported by a recent study conducted by the National Association for College Admission Counseling in which 80 percent of the colleges indicated they placed "considerable importance" on grades in college preparatory courses. The next highest-ranked item, admission test scores, was ranked considerably important by 47 percent. Both are important and may be factors in whether you are accepted. The admission counselors at the colleges you are considering may be able to tell you more about how they weigh your grades and test scores. Ask them!

Question: I did not do well on my admission tests. To what extent will my low scores keep me out of the college I want to attend?

Answer: You appear to have already determined that your scores won't get you into the colleges you're considering. Don't give up so quickly! Admission test scores are one of the criteria considered by colleges as they make admission decisions. In fact, a significant and growing number of colleges do not require admission tests. To obtain a listing of these schools, contact www.fairtest.org.

Test scores are important to those institutions requesting them, but not as important as your achievement in college preparatory studies. If you truly believe your scores are not reflective of the type of work you have done or are capable of doing, attach a note to your application that presents your case and ask your counselor to mention it in his or her recommendation.

Question: How does one select a test preparation program?

Answer: Choosing a test preparation course is best done by obtaining the first-hand evaluation of students who have participated in the programs. Increasingly schools and school districts are offering quality test prep programs for free or for fees far below the commercial competition. Because most of the commercial test prep firms make similar claims about how much they will improve your scores, try to base your choice on factors such as teaching approach, time commitment, and cost. Look for a program that fits your particular need, learning style, and schedule. Ask the test prep company if you can observe one of its classes before making a final commitment. Finally, remember that a number of self-help publications and software programs provide similar instruction. You may find some of these materials in your school or community library.

Question: Should I retake the admission test if I received low scores?

Answer: Like so many aspects of the college admission process, this is a very individual matter and a general response to your question is difficult. If you truly believe that you can do better, by all means register and take the test again. If the colleges you are applying to accept either test, you may also wish to take the other test (ACT vs. SAT or vice versa). Whatever your personal decision, don't allow the improvement of your test scores to become an obsession, one that generates undue stress and affects your academic progress in a negative manner. Your school counselor may have some valuable guidance on the retake issue. Talk to her or him.

Student Exercise 14.1

CREATING YOUR ADMISSION TEST SCHEDULE

Meet with your counselor and consult the administration calendars for those tests that you wish to take as a part of your preparation to apply for college. Make certain you register in accordance with deadlines and meet any other requirements. As you complete each test and receive the results, update this form.

Test	Date	Completed	Results received	Results forwarded to college(s)

CHAPTER 15

Admission Essays: Put Forth Your Best Effort

How important is the essay? How does the college use the essay in making admission decisions? Like most other admission criteria, the weight given to the essay will vary from institution to institution. However, if the college requires an essay, you must treat it with importance and use it as an opportunity to strengthen your application for admission.

A great deal of the college application process is controlled by the questions asked by the college in its application and your ability to answer those questions in a manner that suggests that you're the kind of student they are seeking to admit. They ask. You answer.

Your opportunities to be creative in your response to the college application process are somewhat limited. If the college requires or recommends an interview, you will be able to put a face and a personality with the application, academic transcript, and test scores. But, while a limited number of colleges require interviews, a significant number ask students to write essays or provide writing samples.

While the essay is first a measure of your writing abilities, it also provides insight into your intelligence, expressiveness, and thinking skills. Like the interview, the essay provides you with an opportunity to answer unasked questions and to communicate directly with the educators and officials who have a voice in your admission.

Preparing Your Best Essay or Writing Sample

In preparing the essay that accompanies your college application, consider the following:

1. Talk to college students you know about their essay writing experiences and the subjects about which they were asked to write. This will provide some sense of the challenge you'll find before you.
2. Set aside some specific time to organize your thoughts and do the actual writing and editing of the essay. Avoid times when school and social activities are extremely demanding. The summer after your junior year or the early part of the senior year is the best time to tackle this project.
3. Make certain that you understand the essay assignment, directions (e.g., length), and respond appropriately. Some topics are open-ended and allow you reasonable freedom in shaping your response. Others are more structured and ask you to address a specific issue or topic.
4. If the essay is autobiographical, begin by developing an audit of your relevant personal traits and experiences. Be reflective without being boastful.
5. Follow the practices that have worked for you in writing essays, compositions, and research papers in high school:

   Develop an outline.
   Determine the best format to present your message.
   Prepare a draft.
   Review and edit the draft for grammar, spelling, punctuation, and word usage.
   Evaluate your writing style and treatment of the topic.
   Rewrite and edit as necessary.
   Type, proofread, and prepare for submission.

6. Critique your final draft. Did you address the topic? Were you thorough? Did you provide the proper details? Does it flow well? Is it interesting and focused? Does it hold the reader's attention throughout? Have you conveyed your personal position or feelings about the topic?
7. Ask others for their impressions of your draft essay, but do not ask them to write or rewrite your essay. The essay is to be an example of your creativity and the work needs to come from you.
8. Essays are read by human beings, people who read hundreds (or thousands) of essays. Be sure that yours is "reader friendly."

   College essay readers are looking for thoughtful and sincere content, creative expression, and good writing technique. When you've reach that point, put down your pen, or back away from the keyboard. You have a quality essay!

Note: With the addition of a writing test to the recent revisions of the ACT and SAT tests, some applicants are now substituting this activity for the essay-writing portion of their admission application. Find out how the colleges you are considering are dealing with this issue.

Frequently Asked Questions

Question: What is the most common mistake applicants make in writing their admission essay?

Answer: Too many essay writers read too much into the assignment. They attempt to prepare an essay they think the reader wants to read. Be yourself—be original and you will prepare an excellent essay.

Question: Several colleges I'm considering have requested an essay. Why do they have this requirement and how will the essay influence my chances of admission?

Answer: While the essay is first a measure of your writing abilities, it also provides the college with insight into your intelligence, expressiveness, and thinking skills. Like the interview, the essay provides you an opportunity to answer unasked questions and to communicate directly with the educators and officials who have a voice in your admission. View the essay as an avenue to admission, not an obstacle.

Question: Can you give me some tips on writing the college essay?

Answer: Follow the practices that have worked for you in writing essays, compositions, and research papers in high school. Begin by setting aside some quiet time to organize your thoughts and perform the actual writing and editing of your essay. Be certain you understand fully the essay assignment and directions. Carefully proofread your work for grammar, spelling, word usage, and punctuation and critique it for content, thoroughness, detail, and flow. And finally, you may wish to have your parents or a friend read the essay for clarity and completeness.

Question: If the admission essay is optional, should I submit one?

Answer: Anything "optional" in the college application requirements should be weighed carefully. If you feel that submitting an essay will strengthen your overall application or give the admission officer or committee an opportunity to see a piece of you that is not visible in the remainder of the application, then you would be wise to submit the essay. However, if you don't feel that submitting an essay would influence your application positively, then it's best to exclude it.

CHAPTER 16

Narrowing Options: Deciding Where to Apply

You've engineered an effective exploration campaign and now know a whole lot more about the colleges you're considering and the educational opportunities they present. Along the way some new colleges were added to the list. Some were removed.

There are more than thirty-five hundred two- and four-year colleges in the United States. You have placed a small number of these institutions under your personal microscope. That intense examination has produced a refined list of colleges and universities. Now you must study that list (possibly narrowing it even more) and begin the formal application phase of the high school to college transition.

At this point, a number of new questions emerge. How many applications should I submit? What do the colleges need to know about me in order to consider my candidacy for admission? What are my chances of admission? What is the admission competition like this year? Are there ways that I can increase the odds that I will be admitted?

Review the refined list with respect to those factors that you deem important in the selection of your college. Two rules should guide this final review:

Rule Number One—Your objective has not been to find a single college, but rather the colleges that meet your selection criteria. Surely, you have your favorite or favorites, but try not to be so exclusive in this refinement process that you omit viable options. In other words, there is no solitary "right" college; there should be a number of right colleges.

Rule Number Two—Don't apply to any college that you would not attend if offered admission. If the exploration process has taught you anything, it should have helped you to define your educational goals and how the various colleges measure up to the criteria that you feel are important.

You can address Rule Number Two by answering the following questions: Is the college the right place for you to learn? Will you feel comfortable there as a student and member of the campus community? Is the college affordable or will the financial aid offered make it affordable? If the answer to these questions is yes, move the college forward on your consideration list. If no, consider removing it.

Filing Multiple Admission Applications

Counselors and admission officers recommend that you file multiple college applications, but they do not always agree on the number. Most suggest that three to five applications will be sufficient to vary your exposure and enhance your chances of admission to more than one college.

Those institutions should include (1) "safe" colleges where you are highly likely to gain admission, (2) colleges where you have about a 50–50 chance of admission, and (3) "reach" colleges where admission will depend on the level of competition that particular year.

Many students file a single application and are successful. Some file many more than the number recommended above. A recent survey by UCLA's Higher Education Research Institute revealed that 42 percent of American college freshmen submitted applications to three to five colleges, 29 percent applied to only one or two schools, and 28 percent submitted applications to six or more schools.

Your need for financial assistance may dictate that you file additional applications to expose your academic qualifications to a broader range of colleges and the aid options they present. Remember, too, that there are fees associated with each college application and filing frivolous applications can be expensive.

You will improve your chances of admission by applying to institutions whose admission standards mesh with your academic qualifications and personal characteristics. Devote the appropriate commitment and energy, and you will be satisfied with the results.

Frequently Asked Questions

Question: What do most students say influenced them most in selecting a college?

Answer: Consistently, freshman students have identified the following as the most influential characteristics they sought in their future college: (1) academic reputation, (2) graduates get good jobs, (3) opportunity to visit the college before enrolling, and (4) it was the "right" size. You may look for these elements or add your preference to the list.

Question: With so many colleges to choose from, how is it possible to narrow my choices to just one?

Answer: For the purposes of applying, you don't have to narrow your choices to just one. And you would be ill advised to do so. Your task is to find a number of places to continue your education in an environment that is comfortable and suitable to your needs. Admission to a college that is right for you may require that you apply to multiple institutions. Begin early creating a list of things that you are looking for in your future college. Revise the list as your views change and other things become important to you. Hold all of the colleges you examine up to these criteria. Soon a list of suitable colleges will begin to emerge.

Question: Can I rely on the ratings and ranking systems many magazines use to evaluate colleges?

Answer: Several magazines publish top 100–style lists of colleges. These represent more of the self-help resources that have invaded our culture. Many counselors feel that such ratings have limited value because they are highly subjective. For example, a college may receive an overall low ranking, although it may have a top-notch journalism program that's ideal for many students. Rankings should only supplement your thorough examination of a college. From a college admission perspective, a college is "best" or "worst" only in relation to the needs of the future student.

Question: A friend told me that I should apply to a couple of safety schools? What is a safety school?

Answer: As students narrow their list of colleges, they often include one or two colleges to which they're almost certain to be accepted—commonly referred to as safety schools. If you choose to apply to a safety school, make sure it is one you would want to attend if you are admitted. In other words, don't apply to a safety school just because it's safe.

Question: Are there any specific advantages to applying to in-state versus out-of-state colleges?

Answer: Applying as a state resident to a public university will qualify the student for in-state tuition rates, a reduction that can be significant both annually and over the length of time it takes you to earn a degree. Some financial aid can only be obtained if applied to fees at in-state institutions. While public university costs are usually lower than private institution costs, nonresidents can expect to pay higher costs. All costs at private institutions (in-state or out-of-state) may be offset, however, by the generosity of the grants and scholarships that are available.

Question: I've heard that colleges have a profile of the students they know will enroll if accepted. How will this affect my application?

Answer: The common student practice of applying to multiple safety schools is one that is under considerable scrutiny by the colleges that had previously accepted these students, who then opted for another institution. A growing number of colleges have been rejecting or wait-listing applicants whom they suspect have selected them as a safeguard.

Through personal interviews, colleges try to gauge a student's interest in attending and weed out those who are less than enthusiastic. They will accept an eager student with slightly lower academic qualifications over a less interested one with stronger qualifications. You can increase your chances of admission by being sincere and genuine in all of your dealings with the colleges that really interest you.

Question: What should be some of my concerns if I'm thinking about a community college and then transferring to a four-year school?

Answer: Choosing a community college is not any different than choosing a four-year college or university. If your goal is to transfer after two years, then you have the added responsibility of making certain you take classes that will provide credits that the four-year college will accept. Many community colleges and universities have prearranged these course approvals through articulation agreements, resulting in the development of common course descriptions and academic standards designed specifically to aid the eventual transfer student. If you're considering the transfer option, you should seek the advice of an admission counselor at a four-year institution or the personal advice of a student who has been through the experience. Many colleges have one or more counselors who are specifically assigned to work with transfer applicants.

Question: What are the requirements that I must complete in order to play sports at the collegiate level?

Answer: The National Collegiate Athletic Association (NCAA) has had eligibility standards in effect for some time. These requirements represent a mix of grades in core academic courses with scores on the ACT and SAT admission tests. Your counselor or coach can review the requirements with you.

A list of core courses and other information for college-bound student-athletes and parents can be found at www.ncaa.org/wps/ncaa?ContentID=263. This information is contained in a special guide, *NCAA Guide for the College-Bound Student-Athlete*. Prospective student-athletes can review eligibility standards, recruiting calendars, and other information at the NCAA website (www.ncaa.org). In addition, you can call the NCAA Eligibility Hotline at 1-877-262-1492 to hear recorded messages and request information.

Question: I think I'm a talented soccer player playing on an "average" high school team. How can I get the attention of college coaches and possibly win an athletic scholarship?

Answer: First, you must realize that the competition for athletic scholarships in any sport is extremely high and the number of scholarships awarded to college student-athletes is minimal when compared to the number of high school students in any given sport. Work with your high school coach in an attempt to identify the collegiate level of competition and some of the colleges where your soccer talents might be appropriate. High school and college coaches participate in networks to share information about prospects, and your coach may be able to connect you with some college coaches. Your coach may also be able to forward videotapes that display your soccer skills. Finally, when you talk with admission counselors or visit colleges make known your interest in the sport and try to connect personally with the coaches and players of the college team.

Question: What are the advantages of attending a historically black college or university?

Answer: Students attending one of the nation's more than one hundred black colleges or universities find an academic and social environment that emphasizes African American history and culture. Further, they often find role models in the faculty, administrators, and upper-class students of color that they will be less likely to find on other campuses. The historically black colleges and universities, or HBCUs as they are often called, have a rich tradition of providing quality educational experiences and presenting an alternative learning and living environment for the African American student. HBCUs also help in creating a student bond or kinship that many suggest is not present at more diverse institutions. A campus visit and interaction with enrolled students is certain to point out many of these unique characteristics.

Question: How can I find out about colleges that offer special programs for students with learning disabilities?

Answer: Discovering whether a college can address a specific learning disability should be one of the questions you pose during the exploration process. Direct these questions to the admission counselors or seek the answers from the student service professionals (e.g., tutors, therapists) responsible for working directly with disabled students. You may also wish to check out the resources of the National Clearinghouse on Postsecondary Education for Individuals with Disabilities at George Washington University. Visit www.heath.gwu.edu and you will find the *Information from HEATH* newsletter, resource guides, and other helpful tools.

Question: Our local newspaper recently ran a series of stories about career school scams. How can I avoid enrolling at a bad school?

Answer: Once you have found a career or occupational study program that interests you, evaluate it in two ways. First, check to see if the school is accredited by the Accrediting Commission of Career Schools and Colleges of Technology. You can review their list of accredited institutions at www.accsct.org/Directory-Search.aspx.

Second, ask current students or recent graduates to tell you about their educational experiences. If you get positive responses to these two measures, then it is likely the school is a bona fide institution, one capable of providing you with a quality education.

Question: Are national student award and recognition programs highly regarded by college admission officers?

Answer: If you compete and are successful in academic competitions, such as the Intel Science Talent Search or the USA Today All Academic Team, these honors are certain to catch the eye of the admission officer assigned to read your application. The critical element in each of these and similar recognition programs is that real academic and scholarship competition is involved. Some recognition programs are nothing more than individual students submitting academic and extracurricular data for inclusion in a registry or publication. This type of recognition carries little or no weight in the admission process. To add insult, you'll also be pestered endlessly to buy a copy of the directory containing your name.

Student Exercise 16.1

EXAMINING THE ADMISSION COMPETITION

One of the best indicators of whether you will be admitted to a college is how you stack up against the students that institution typically admits. Similar academic qualifications and personal experiences will be viewed positively and often result in admission. This information is contained in a freshman profile that is published in college guidebooks and viewbooks and sometimes posted on the college website. Students can also examine the range of admission test scores of the most recently admitted freshman class. Counselors and admission officers can also provide information for this exercise.

College _____

Percentage of applicants that are admitted   _____

Percentage of admitted students that enroll   _____

Senior class standing

Percentage in upper 1/10th of class   _____

Percentage in upper 1/4 of class   _____

Percentage in upper 1/2 of class   _____

Admission test scores

Range of ACT composite scores   _____

Range of SAT verbal scores   _____

Range of SAT math scores   _____

Range of SAT writing scores   _____

Admission competition level

_____ Highly selective   _____ Moderately selective   _____ Not selective

List below any information you have received from students, teachers, or your counselor regarding the academic competitiveness of the college.

_____

_____

_____

_____

Repeat this exercise for each of the colleges where you are considering applying.

Student Exercise 16.2

RANKING THE MOST IMPORTANT COLLEGE CHARACTERISTICS

Review your responses to Student Exercise 5.1, College and University Characteristics: Exploring Your Personal Preferences. List up to ten characteristics (e.g., academic reputation, availability of major, college costs, etc.) below that you feel are the most important in your personal college search. As you review college guides and websites, meet with college admission officers, and visit campuses, examine these characteristics carefully as you evaluate each institution. For this exercise, insert the names of three colleges that you're seriously considering and study the extent to which each institution possesses the characteristics you deem important.

Record your evaluation according to the following scale:

+ Strong presence of the characteristic
O Modest or limited presence of the characteristic
− Absence of the characteristic

College Selection Characteristics	College #1	College#2	College #3
1. _____	_____	_____	_____
2. _____	_____	_____	_____
3. _____	_____	_____	_____
4. _____	_____	_____	_____
5. _____	_____	_____	_____
6. _____	_____	_____	_____
7. _____	_____	_____	_____
8. _____	_____	_____	_____
9. _____	_____	_____	_____
10. _____	_____	_____	_____

Student Exercise 16.3

THE FINAL REVIEW: CREATING YOUR APPLICATION LIST

Insert the names of the colleges (in any order) that you continue to consider below. To the right, offer an appraisal as to whether the college is a "safe" or a "reach" school. A safe school is one that has a history of admitting students with your type of academic and personal credentials. A reach school suggests that your qualifications are more borderline and the competition for admission is greater. Don't create a list made up entirely of reach schools. Your counselor can help you with this appraisal. Finally, list three characteristics (e.g., strong journalism school, friendly atmosphere, affordable, etc.) that have impressed you about the college. These characteristics will be influential in the decisions you are about to make.

College: _____ ____ Safe ____ Reach

Characteristics that have impressed me during the search process:

1. _____

2. _____

3. _____

College: _____ ____ Safe ____ Reach

Characteristics that have impressed me during the search process:

1. _____

2. _____

3. _____

College: _____ ____ Safe ____ Reach

Characteristics that have impressed me during the search process:

1. _____

2. _____

3. _____

College: _____ ____ Safe ____ Reach

Characteristics that have impressed me during the search process:

1. _____

2. _____

3. _____

College: _____ ____ Safe ____ Reach

Characteristics that have impressed me during the search process:

1. _____

2. _____

3. _____

College: _____ ____ Safe ____ Reach

Characteristics that have impressed me during the search process:

1. _____

2. _____

3. _____

College: _____ ____ Safe ____ Reach

Characteristics that have impressed me during the search process:

1. _____

2. _____

3. _____

Student Exercise: 16.4

APPLICATION LIST:
COLLEGES WHERE YOU WILL SUBMIT APPLICATIONS

Once you have completed this exercise, review the list and the characteristics you have identified for each college. Next rank the colleges (1 through ?) in the order of personal preference. Note: After you have given full consideration to college costs and the availability of student financial aid, you may need to review your ranking.

1. _____

2. _____

3. _____

4. _____

5. _____

6. _____

7. _____

8. _____

9. _____

10. _____

CHAPTER 17

The College Application: Making It Work for You

It's application time. On your desk are a number of envelopes containing application forms, financial aid forms, instruction sheets, and related materials. At first glance, that pile of application materials may appear intimidating.

Like all other aspects of the school-to-college transition, the application phase can produce some anxious, confusing, and stressful times. Coming at the beginning of the senior year, it competes with your efforts to sustain or accelerate your academic efforts and enjoy an extracurricular and social life. You can maintain control by doing the following:

1. Gather all of the forms, instruction sheets, and support materials that are needed to apply for admission and financial aid to the colleges that you are interested in attending. Have everything that you need before you embark on the application submission journey. If the college will accept the Common Application, you may wish to consider that option and use this form for multiple applications. Visit the Common Application website at www.common-app.org to access the online form.

2. Review all of the applications and create a checklist of what needs to be done, who does it, and when it needs to be completed. Determine if the college has an application on their website that you can complete online and transmit electronically or print and send by regular mail.

   Note: If you are applying to a college under an early action, early decision, or restricted early decision plan, the application timetable will be accelerated. Check the college viewbook, website, or with an admission counselor to determine the deadline dates for these special plans.

3. Complete the form(s):

   • Read the entire application form before completing any of the sections.
   • Make copies of the forms and use the copies as worksheets.

- Follow each direction exactly and provide all of the information that is requested. Don't feel compelled or forced to fill in every space on the form. Answer the questions that are relevant to your application.
- Provide accurate and concise answers.
- Prepare a neat application, typing or printing your responses. Edit your responses.

4. Make certain that the required materials accompany the application, including:

- Essays—Review the essay topics and instructions and devote sufficient time to produce your best work.
- Academic records and transcripts—Colleges will want copies of your official academic record and transcript to support your application. Direct this request through your school counselor, registrar, or records officer.
- Recommendations—A couple of in-depth recommendations from people who know you and your abilities and achievements are better than many from those who have a casual familiarity. If a college asks for a specific number or designates the specific recommendation writers, be certain to honor its request. Provide guidelines and timetables to these individuals and don't wait until the last minute to request your recommendations.
- Test scores—Schedule your SAT, ACT, and related testing sessions to allow time (normally six weeks) for score reports to get to the college for proper consideration.
- Interview—If the college requires a personal interview, it is your responsibility to see that it fits into the admission timetable.
- Other materials—The college application lists the information they need to evaluate your application. Don't send extraneous materials (e.g., videos, term papers, newspaper clips, etc.). Most likely, they won't be reviewed.

5. Know the deadline dates and send your applications to the college(s) on time. Procrastination will be your greatest enemy at this stage of the college admission process. Develop an application submission checklist and timetable and stick to them. Should questions arise, consult with your counselor or the college admission/financial aid officers.

Frequently Asked Questions

Question: Is it possible that I could "lose points" with an admission officer because of the appearance of my application?

Answer: An application that is messy or difficult to read will certainly detract from the impression you wish to make. If you and another candidate are competing for a spot in the freshman class and all other aspects of your application are reasonably equal, the scales might be tipped in the favor of the more attractive application. Don't take that chance!

Question: What is the Common Application and how may it be used?

Answer: The Common Application is a single college application that is accepted at approximately three hundred and fifty institutions across the nation. Using the Common Application simplifies the process and reduces the time required because the same information (including essays) can be directed to multiple colleges. Over the years some students and counselors have questioned whether colleges give preference to students who complete the college's application. The colleges participating in this program say "no." Print and disk versions of the Common Application can be obtained from your school counselor. The online form is posted at www.commonapp.org/CommonApp/default.aspx.

Question: How many applications for admission should I submit?

Answer: Unless you are very confident in your abilities and your study of the various colleges, filing just one application can be somewhat risky. Most students file multiple applications so that they can increase their exposures to include both safety (you stand a strong chance of being admitted) and reach (you stand a moderate to slim chance of being admitted) schools. The number of applications is not as important as the quality of the exploration and decision making that preceded them.

Question: What are the most common mistakes that high school students make in preparing and filing their college applications?

Answer: Many students err at the beginning by failing to read the entire application package before starting to complete it. Admission officers also cite incompleteness, sloppiness, and missing deadlines as common mistakes made by the applicants. With the exception of situations involving an essay or interview, the application is all that the college has to evaluate your candidacy, and you should take considerable care that your application is the best "you" that you can present.

Question: I'm considering sending off more than five admission applications. What am I looking at in application fees?

Answer: Recent research indicates that most fees for filing college admission applications fall in the $25 neighborhood. Five applications will run $125 or more.

Fees for filing applications at public institutions and two-year colleges typically run a little less than private and four-year institutions. More than three-fourths of all institutions have a fee waiver policy for those students who claim the fee creates a financial hardship.

Question: I'm considering a college that requests that I interview with a representative of the institution. What is the purpose of this interview?

Answer: Colleges request interviews for a couple of reasons. Some interviews are part of the evaluation process, and the interviewer (staff or alumni representative) will prepare a report that will become part of your application file. Other interviews are informational and give you an opportunity to ask questions in a private and personal setting. You will need to ask the admission officer how the interview will be used. Whatever the purpose, the key to a successful interview is to be yourself and go prepared with questions that are important to your application and eventual enrollment. Not all colleges use the interview in an evaluative sense. They use it to meet you and answer your questions on a more personal level.

Question: The colleges I'm interested in have all requested personal recommendations. How will they be used?

Answer: College recommendations that are prepared by teachers, counselors, or others represent an important aspect of the admission decision process for colleges requesting them. Admission counselors read recommendations to gain insight into qualities that are not obvious from objective measures, such as your grade point average or admission test scores. Recommendations reveal personality, motivations for learning, and philosophy. They give an admission officer a mental snapshot of who you are. Although it is not the most important item in your application, a favorable recommendation is a welcome addition. Submit the number requested or recommended on the application. Don't overkill with too many!

Question: Who should I get to write my college recommendation letters?

Answer: First and foremost, follow the instructions on the college application regarding any recommendation letters the college requires. One or two in-depth recommendations from people (e.g., counselor, teachers, coaches) who know you and your abilities and achievements are better than a handful from those who have a casual familiarity. When approaching your counselor or teachers, provide guidelines and timetables they can follow in getting the recommendations to the colleges. Don't wait to the last minute to ask for their assistance.

Question: Last year a student in my high school sent a videotape of one of her drama performances along with her college application? Does this help?

Answer: College admission officers, charged with the evaluation of hundreds, sometimes thousands of admission applications, do not have the time to view student videos, and they generally discourage students from submitting such items. However, there are exceptions. Many schools of art, music, and performing arts require students to provide samples of their work and experiences, often in the form of a portfolio, tape, or video. Coaches, too, often like to see videos or films of athletic performances. Read the application materials carefully to determine the policies at each institution.

Student Exercise 17.1

THE COLLEGE ADMISSION APPLICATION CHECKLIST

As you move through the final stages of the admission application process, it is important to organize the various tasks according to a timetable that keeps you in total control of the process. The following checklist will keep you on schedule throughout the application submission period. Ask your counselor to review the checklist to make sure that you have identified all of the tasks that you must complete and you have recorded the correct deadlines. Note: If you are filing under any early decision or early action plan, adjust all completion dates according to the particular plan.

Many colleges permit students to complete admission applications online. Often the submission process is controlled electronically and applicants are guided step by step through the entire process. It is wise to print out a copy of all electronically submitted applications for your admission records and as proof of your submission.

College or University: _____

Application task	Date required	Date completed
1. Reviewed college application form and filing requirements.	_____	_____
2. Requested transcript be forwarded to college by high school guidance office or registrar.	_____	_____
3. Requested letter of recommendation be prepared and forwarded to college by the following individuals:	_____	_____
_____	_____	_____
_____	_____	_____
_____	_____	_____
4. Requested test scores be forwarded to college.	_____	_____
5. Completed essay (if required).	_____	_____
6. Scheduled interview (if required or recommended).	_____	_____

7. Other, specify below:

_____   _____   _____

_____   _____   _____

_____   _____   _____

8. Completed all application requirements.   _____   _____

Note: Make additional copies of this form for each college application.

CHAPTER 18

Understanding College Costs

Paying the college bills has become an expensive proposition for the American student and his or her family. Like most items that we purchase in America, college costs have risen consistently. Over the past two decades, these costs outpaced inflation, and the same is expected to occur for the foreseeable future.

Today, according to an annual study conducted by College Board, four years at a private college (including tuition, fees, room and board) can average between $125,000 and $140,000. The cost of four years at a public college or university (including tuition, fees, room and board) ranges from $60,000 to $90,000 for resident students. Out-of-state students will pay more.

Another factor to consider is the ability of the student to complete his or her studies in four years. The time it takes to attain a degree has been steadily creeping upward and this means additional costs for the fifth or sixth year. At the same time, more and more students are competing for the billions of dollars in financial assistance made available by government, institutions, and private sources to students each year in postsecondary education. Recent studies by the U.S. Department of Education report that seven in ten college students will use some form of financial aid before they graduate.

All of these conditions warrant students' and their families' understanding just what they are paying for and exercising control when options exist. College costs fall into two categories: fixed and controllable.

Fixed Costs

These costs are the same for all students. They include

tuition,
room and board, and
student fees.

Tuition is the cost of your education and is set by the institution or by the governing authority overseeing the institution or system of higher education. Room and board costs are fixed if the student is required to live on campus, a situation that is often the case for first-year students. Student fees range from the activities fee (providing access to athletic and cultural events) to laboratory and library fees.

Note: A number of colleges have experimented with fixed or limited-increase tuition plans. In these situations, students entering college at a particular point know the cost of tuition and the adjustments they can expect to see during their total enrollment period.

Controllable Costs

These are the costs for which the student can exercise some degree of spending authority. They include

books, materials, and fees (i.e., Internet access, etc.),
personal expenses,
transportation, and
room and board (off campus).

Book costs can be controlled somewhat by the acquisition of used books. Personal expenses such as entertainment, clothing, and sundries are influenced by preference, need, and consumption rates. Think about the items (e.g., shampoo, snacks, stamps, etc.) you need and consume today. When you get to college, the cost of these things will come out of your personal expenses budget.

Transportation between the student's home and the campus and other travel costs are affected by the method of transportation that one uses to get back and forth and how often the student travels. Room and board costs can be controlled when the student resides off campus or has variable campus meal plans available.

Given the range of expenses and the limited ability that students have to exercise control, it is important that costs, aid opportunities, and options be fully examined and understood. Cost should never be used as the factor or criterion that guides exploration, and no college should ever be excluded from consideration due to cost until the student knows what type of financial assistance package might be assembled by the financial aid office.

Understanding college costs is only half of the information that students and their families must possess. You must also understand the college student financial aid system and the various forms of assistance that are available. It is information you won't regret researching.

Frequently Asked Questions

Question: How much does college really cost these days?

Answer: A recent study by the College Board indicates that the average college costs per year at four-year institutions as $13,589 at public and $32,307 at private colleges. These figures reflected tuition and fees, books and supplies, room and board, and transportation costs. The public average was based on an in-state resident student. Remember, these are averages. Some will be somewhat lower and others much higher.

Question: Are college costs in any way controllable or does everyone pay the same amount?

Answer: College costs can be controlled to a limited extent. While tuition, fees, and room and board, for the most part, are the same for all students, you might be able to modify your living arrangements or meal plan to control costs somewhat. Many of the things you pay for are based on frequency or consumption. These include books where you can save by purchasing used textbooks and personal expenses such as movies, long-distance telephone calls, snacks, dry cleaning, stamps, and related items. Transportation costs from college to home can also be controlled by the frequency of the visits and the mode of transportation used. If you are given the option or opportunity to live off campus and this is something you wish to do, you will find housing costs vary considerably in each college community.

Question: I need to go to a college my family and I can afford. How strongly should cost influence my decision?

Answer: Cost should be a consideration only after you look at whether the college is the right place for you academically and socially. In other words, will the institution present you with academic challenges you can live up to? Next, will you enjoy the social setting and lifestyle offered by the college and the community? The cost of college will play heavily on your eventual decision, but don't make it the only or first ingredient in your examination. Remember, many financial aid programs are available to help you meet college expenses. Try to get an idea of the aid you might be eligible for as you weigh the financial factor in your selection process.

Question: Have colleges ever been known to cut their costs or offer discounts?

Answer: Unlike commercial establishments, colleges do not have sales and bargain days. This, however, does not mean that everyone pays the same. Many higher-priced private colleges have found ways to use institutional aid to reduce the costs for students with financial needs that they want to enroll. Billions of dollars in institutional aid is awarded each year by the colleges themselves. Such aid is far more limited or nonexistent at public institutions where costs are substantially lower. Since each institution is spending its own resources, the criteria for getting this assistance will vary, but demonstrated need is a common criteria.

Student Exercise 18.1

DETERMINING COLLEGE COSTS:
A PERSONAL BUDGETING PROCESS

Use the spaces below to identify the costs associated with those colleges that you are interested in attending. Accurate college tuition, room and board, and related costs can be found in the literature distributed by each institution. Since costs fluctuate greatly from year to year, make certain that you have current figures.

Expenses	College	College	College
Tuition and fees			
Room and board			
Books, supplies, materials, etc.			
Living expenses			
Transportation			
Other expenses, specify:			
Total college budget			

CHAPTER 19

Types and Sources of Student Financial Aid

Education after high school is a major investment for the family and financing higher education today has become a major challenge. Part of the challenge is to learn how the financial aid system works and the degree to which the various forms of student financial aid will offset the rising costs.

The financial aid system in American higher education operates according to the following basic principle: Students and their families contribute to the cost of college to the extent or level they are able. The difference between their ability to contribute and the cost of going to college is referred to as "need." Consider the following formula:

Cost of college – student/family contribution = financial aid eligibility

Since much of the student assistance in this nation comes from federal sources, guidelines established by the Congress and administered by the U.S. Department of Education provide the structure for many of the other student financial aid programs and policies. To qualify for federal assistance and for much of the aid offered by related sources, students must demonstrate need.

Even though college costs may vary, the family contribution remains constant. The student's financial aid eligibility increases as the cost increases, one important reason that students should not exclude colleges from consideration simply on the basis of cost.

There are three basic types of federal student financial aid:

Grants and gift aid—Grants are gift aid and do not have to be repaid. The amount of the federal grant will vary from year to year, dependent on the funds that have been appropriated for the grant programs.

Work-study—Work-study is student assistance in the form of employment at your college. This part-time employment provides you an opportunity to earn money (at least at current federal minimum wage levels) to offset the cost of your schooling.

Student loans—Loans enable students and parents to borrow funds to meet educational costs. These loans must be repaid with interest.

To order free publications and learn more about the federal student aid programs, call 1-800-4FEDAID or visit www.ed.gov.

Beyond the federal aid programs, students will find financial aid available from state governments, private sources, and from the colleges themselves. State governments typically require demonstrated need and residency, but may have other eligibility criteria as well.

Private scholarship programs are offered by corporations, public service, and fraternal organizations, foundations, labor unions, and other philanthropic groups. These are both merit- and need-based. Once you have narrowed the list of colleges to a reasonable number, inquire as to the availability of scholarships and grants from those institutions. Colleges differ in their ability to meet the needs of their students. High-cost colleges typically put together larger student aid packages, usually combining grants, work-study, and loans.

Students and families need to be aware of the terms under which aid is offered and any requirements (e.g., maintenance of a specific grade point average) for its continuance. Because of the perception that only the neediest families qualify for assistance many students do not even apply for assistance. All families should examine the various sources of aid and determine the extent to which they can and should participate.

School counselors can provide general information about sources and types of financial assistance and often know about special scholarships and awards that are unique to the school, community, or region. College financial aid officers are experts in the federal, state, and institution programs and can provide details about the lending opportunities and terms offered at commercial banks.

Frequently Asked Questions

Question: Help me to understand the purpose of financial aid. Isn't it designed to help students with considerable need pay for college?

Answer: Financial aid comes in many different forms. You are correct in assuming that a considerable amount of financial aid is targeted at students who wouldn't be able to go to college without this help. But that number has risen steadily as college costs have increased. Today, as many as two-thirds of the students on many campuses are receiving some form of financial aid. Aid based on financial circumstances is referred to as need-based aid. Aid that is awarded on the basis of individual talent or personal accomplishment is known as merit aid.

Often merit assistance does not take need into account and can be awarded to any student meeting the criteria. In other instances, financial aid may be awarded on the basis of both need and merit. Since some merit-based awards are competitive, you will need to conduct a thorough study of these sources and file the necessary applications.

Question: How dependent have students become on financial aid?

Answer: When freshman college students around the nation were asked in the American College Freshman study if they felt they had sufficient funds to pay for their college experience, nearly four in ten (39 percent) expressed confidence that they did. Slightly more than half (52 percent) said they had some concern about their ability to pay their bills, and 10 percent expressed major concern that they would have enough funds to complete college. This same study indicated a growing number of students expect they will have to get a job while in college to help pay the bills.

Question: I'm confused about just who makes financial aid available to students. Can you help me?

Answer: College student financial aid comes from basically three sources: government (federal and state), institutions, and the private sector. Federal and state aid is available in the form of grants, work-study programs, and scholarships: each having different need and eligibility requirements. Institutional aid represents those dollars that a particular college has to disperse to aid students it is hoping to enroll. Finally, a considerable amount of assistance is made available by corporations, foundations, philanthropic groups, and service organizations to students meeting their award criteria. While much of the aid from the latter group is awarded through national competition, some local sources restrict their aid to students from a given high school, residents of a particular community, or children of their employees.

Your school counselor, librarian, and the financial aid officer at the college you're considering will be a valuable source of information about these programs. You should also consider using College Board's Scholarship Search, a computer software program that will allow you to search for scholarships and get a head start on calculating the family contribution you and your parents will have to apply to the cost of your college expenses before some forms of financial aid will be available.

Question: The college I want to attend is offering me less in my financial aid package than another college. Is there any way for me to use that offer to bargain with my first choice?

Answer: At the risk of making the process sound like purchasing a used car, the current college admission and financial aid climate offers the talented student more opportunity for negotiation than he or she might believe. There is nothing wrong with letting your first choice college know about the financial aid package being offered by another institution. Private colleges, for example, have some latitude in shaping their aid packages, and, in some instances, you may see an adjustment to your original offer. Public colleges will not have the same flexibility.

Don't ever present your situation as a "match it or I'm outta here" kind of ultimatum. There are many qualified individuals seeking admission who are just as deserving and in need of the college's aid as you.

Question: An admission officer at a private college told me to look beyond costs to possible financial aid when comparing public and private colleges. What did she mean?

Answer: What the admission officer was saying was that on the surface private colleges often seem twice, sometimes three or four times, as expensive as public colleges. But, private institutions have the ability to put together more flexible and usually larger financial aid packages for the students they hope will enroll. It's important not to remove any college from consideration solely on the basis of cost.

Question: What does "need blind" admission mean?

Answer: The term "need blind" means that the college's admission decision is not based in any way on a person's financial need and that any financial aid decisions are made independently, usually in a different office of the college. A small number of colleges are not need blind and will examine a student's financial status. If his or her need is too great, and the college cannot offer a financial aid package to cover that amount of need, the student may be denied admission. Fortunately for you, a great majority of colleges employ a need blind policy, and, at these schools, your financial status will not influence your chances for admission. If you have a concern, ask the admission office to explain the manner in which decisions are made at their institution.

Question: What is the difference between a scholarship and a grant?

Answer: In the language of a financial aid officer, a scholarship and a grant are basically the same thing. Both are "gift" aid meaning they do not need to be paid back. Some forms of gift aid, however, may require that you meet certain requirements like maintaining a certain grade point average or majoring in a particular field. Make sure you understand any terms or restrictions that are associated with any assistance you receive before you accept the aid.

Question: What are work-study programs and how can I find out about them from the colleges I'm applying to?

Answer: Work-study is a form of need-based financial aid where a student may earn money by working on campus or with an approved off-campus employer. Work-study is usually packaged with grants, scholarships, and loans to reduce costs and make the college experience more affordable. Students considering any type of employment need to be sensitive to balancing study and work. Otherwise, the work experience can have a negative effect on classroom performance and can easily interrupt one's academic program. The financial aid office at the college will have information about work-study opportunities and their eligibility requirements.

Question: When a college offers me a financial aid package, is it good for all four years or is my situation evaluated each year?

Answer: Some of the scholarships you may be offered will be good for the entire four years. Some may not. Be certain that you understand the duration of the gift and the conditions (e.g., maintaining a certain grade point average) under which you accept it. The Pell Grant program, the largest federal student assistance program, is based on need and your situation will be evaluated each year to determine your eligibility. Be leery of institutions that "front load" your assistance to get you to enroll and then leave you to your own devices, such as taking out student loans, to pay for the remaining years.

Question: I've seen the term "family contribution" in several books about financial aid. What does it mean?

Answer: You may be referring to the "expected family contribution" or EFC. This is the amount, determined by a congressional formula, that a student's family is expected to contribute toward the cost of attending college. It is factored into all federal student assistance awards. The EFC is printed on the front of the Student Aid Report (SAR) that you will receive following the processing of the Free Application for Federal Student Aid (FAFSA). This information is also forwarded to colleges.

Question: Are competitive scholarships worth pursuing?

Answer: When your abilities, achievements, and interests fall in line with a particular scholarship program and the scholarship looks like it was meant for you, go after it with vigor and enthusiasm. Unfortunately, this will not always be the case. If you knew the number of students competing for some scholarship programs, you might consider buying a lottery ticket instead. If the scholarship requires completion of a tedious application or completion of some other requirement (e.g., essay), you may wish to consider the yield versus the effort you must expend. When you research scholarships, try to determine the number of scholarships awarded in comparison to the number of applicants. You will soon recognize that some scholarships are next to impossible to get. Don't forget the scholarships awarded right in your high school and community. They may not be large dollar awards, but they won't attract thousands of applicants either.

Student Exercise 19.1

EXAMINING THE AVAILABILITY OF FINANCIAL AID

Take time to talk with your counselor and the admission and financial aid representatives of the college(s) you are interested in attending. Spend some time reviewing the financial aid guidebooks and computer disks in your guidance office or library. From those discussions and your research, create a list of scholarships, grants, work-study programs, and loans. In the space below, make a list of financial aid opportunities for which you wish to get applications and eligibility criteria.

Source	Type of Assistance	Comments
Federal/National		

_____

_____

_____

_____

_____

State

_____

_____

_____

_____

Local

_____

_____

_____

_____

Institution

_____

_____

_____

_____

_____

Private

_____

_____

_____

_____

_____

CHAPTER 20

Making Financial Aid Forms Work for You

If completing the collection of college admission forms you've assembled wasn't enough, you'll soon discover that financial aid application forms will require equal time and attention. Unless you're one of the third of college students not receiving some form of financial assistance, you will need to file original forms and update or refile them each year you wish to remain an aid recipient.

The process begins by making certain that you have the right forms. Some will be available from your high school guidance office. Others will come directly from the college or from the agency, firm, or organization making the award. Other forms, like loan applications, must be obtained from the banks or lending institutions. It's a good idea to ask for financial aid forms at the time you are gathering your admission applications.

Once assembled, it is always a good idea to review all of the forms to determine what information you will need to respond to the questions. Since financial aid is often based on need, many of the questions will address family financial matters. Your parents need to be involved in their completion and must attest to their accuracy.

To be considered for the federal student aid programs (e.g., Federal Pell Grants and Federal Family Education Loans), a student must complete the Free Application for Federal Student Aid (FAFSA). This application collects financial aid and other information used to calculate the Expected Family Contribution (EFC) that ultimately determines the student's eligibility for aid.

Since eligibility for the federal programs serves as the basis for other financial aid programs, the FAFSA is the first and, in many cases, the only financial aid form the student will complete. The information that accompanies the FAFSA will direct the applicant regarding the application processing cycle.

The U.S. Department of Education makes the FAFSA available in both paper and electronic formats. To complete the electronic version, visit www.fafsa

.ed.gov. You will also find a number of student and parent resources and a financial aid estimator (www.fafsa4caster.ed.gov/) at the Department of Education website. Additionally, you can order *The Student Guide* and *Funding Your Education*, two U.S. Department of Education publications providing current information about federal and related student assistance. Should you need help completing the electronic version of the FAFSA, go to www.studentaid.ed.gov. Further assistance is available by contacting the Federal Student Aid Information Center, PO Box 84, Washington, D.C. 20044, or calling the toll-free federal student aid information number: 1-800-4FEDAID (1-800-433-3243).

Approximately four weeks after submitting the FAFSA, you'll receive a Student Aid Report (SAR). The SAR contains the information that you provided on the FAFSA, plus your Expected Family Contribution (EFC). This is the figure that the college will use in determining your eligibility for federal student aid. It is your responsibility to check the SAR and make sure that everything is correct. Also, be certain that your current address is always on file with the U.S. Department of Education.

If you are an applicant for institutional aid, you may be required to complete the CSS/Financial Aid PROFILE® or a college-specific financial aid application. These forms will request information beyond that on the FAFSA, information that the colleges feel is important in their assessment of need. The CSS/Financial Aid PROFILE® can be accessed at the College Board website: www.profileonline.collegeboard.com/index.jsp. The college financial aid officer can tell you what forms will be required to apply for institutional aid and offer any guidance you may need in their completion.

In addition to the FAFSA, CSS/Financial Aid PROFILE®, and college-specific forms, you will need a number of other items when you and your parents sit down to complete this important task. These include: (1) your most recent tax return, (2) your parents' most recent tax return, and (3) other records such as W-2 forms, bank statements, business/farm records, and investment records.

During the process of completing the various forms, make certain that you answer all of the relevant questions with the most current and accurate information. Sign each form (some require both student and parent signatures) and send them off to the appropriate processing agency or office. Be sensitive to deadlines as many scholarships, grants, and institutional awards have cyclical application periods or award the assistance on a first come, first served basis.

Frequently Asked Questions

Question: What are the most critical dates in the financial aid application calendar?

Answer: There are at least two sets of dates, and possibly many others impossible to count, that you will need to learn and juggle as you apply for the various forms of financial aid you might be considering. First, you need to complete and file the Free Application for Federal Student Aid (FAFSA) and the CSS/Financial Aid PROFILE® as early as possible. After that, most of the financial aid deadlines will be those of the colleges and the scholarships or programs to which you are applying. Both the application requirements and filing deadlines for these awards will vary greatly. Your best bet is to put together an admission and financial aid calendar that lists all of the tasks you need to perform. This calendar should include at least three columns; one each for the name of the award, the filing deadline, and the date you want to have the application completed.

Question: Am I required to complete the Free Application for Federal Student Aid if I'm not eligible for federal government assistance?

Answer: The FAFSA is the "rock" upon which most financial aid decisions are built. Whether you feel you are eligible for federal student assistance or not, you should prepare and file a FAFSA as soon after the beginning of January in your senior year as possible. A second form, the CSS/Financial Aid PROFILE® may also be required. After you have submitted an application form to College Scholarship Service, you'll be sent their form requesting family financial details not included on the FAFSA. Unlike the FAFSA, there is a filing fee for the CSS/Financial Aid PROFILE®. The information generated by the FAFSA, the CSS/Financial Aid PROFILE®, and the college's own financial aid application (required by some colleges) will be examined by the financial aid office in determining your personal financial aid package. File these forms as early as possible.

Question: How can I recognize the rip-off schemes of scholarship search firms?

Answer: "If it sounds too good to believe . . . it probably is" is an old adage that has particular relevance here. Services that make outrageous claims like "billions of dollars in financial aid goes unclaimed each year" are worthy of considerable scrutiny before you make payment for services. The best advice for those concerned about fee-charging financial aid services is to exhaust the counseling services of the high school and the college admission and financial aid office before purchasing these services from independent sources.

Many services provide little real help for the fees charged, which can range from $50 to $250 or more for a scholarship search service that you can most likely conduct yourself on the Internet. The Bureau of Consumer Protection and

Federal Trade Commission have established an Internet website where you can learn more about the questionable practices of some of these firms. Visit www.ftc .gov/bcp/conline.edcams/scholarship/cases.shtm. Students and parents can also call the toll-free FTC consumer line at 1-877-FTC-HELP (1-877-382-4357) for additional assistance.

Student Exercise 20.1

FINANCIAL AID APPLICATION CHECKLIST

Much like the admission application process, your applications for scholarships, grants, and other forms of financial aid are going to require specific attention. The following checklist will keep you on schedule throughout this period. Your counselor or a financial aid advisor at the colleges you're considering can also provide guidance in the completion of these forms. As family financial information is usually required on these forms, allow sufficient time for your parents to participate.

Whether you submit a paper or electronic application for financial aid, you need to recognize that some forms must be filed with the federal government, state government, or other national entities that help to determine your eligibility for assistance. Make certain you understand these requirements and the order in which they must be completed. Your application for institutional assistance and some private scholarships could be predicated on those requirements already being met.

Financial Aid Application task	Date required	Date completed
1. Completed and submitted FAFSA.		
2. Completed and submitted CSS/Financial Aid PROFILE®.		
3. Requested federal financial aid report forwarded to college(s).		
4. Requested CSS/Financial Aid PROFILE® report forwarded to college(s).		
5. Completed appropriate state financial aid form(s).		
6. Completed appropriate institution-specific financial aid form(s).		
7. Completed application(s) for work-study programs.		
8. Completed scholarship application form(s) required by the college.		
9. Completed application(s) for private scholarships (national and local).		
10. Other, specify:		

CHAPTER 21

After the Application: What Happens Next?

When the application for admission has been reviewed by a college, one of four actions can result. If you have explored properly and applied to colleges where the students reflect the academic characteristics and personal qualities that you present, there is a strong likelihood that an acceptance letter will find its way to your mailbox.

According to the Higher Education Research Institute, 81 percent of a recent college freshman class said they had been accepted by their first-choice college. And nearly 90 percent were enrolled at either their first or second choice. If offered admission to more than one institution, you have the pleasant (and possibly difficult) task of deciding where you will enroll in the fall.

If an application is not accepted, there are three other outcomes. Let's look at each.

Conditional Admission—A conditional admission means that your admission is dependent upon your meeting some special or additional requirement (e.g., summer study, midyear enrollment). Contact the college admission office directly to make certain you understand the terms of the admission and your time line for meeting these requirements.

Wait-List—If you're wait-listed, you have a right to know the wait-list history of the institution. In other words, how many people typically move from the list to general admission? If you can review the wait-list history for a couple of earlier classes, you'll get some sense of your status and whether you should hold out hope of enrollment. If your applications result in a combination of acceptances and wait-list responses, you'll need to consider these variables as the date approaches for responding to your offers of admission. Again, it is wise to consult with the admission officer(s) and your counselor for interpretation and guidance.

Application Denied—Some students who are denied admission take it upon themselves to appeal the decision, especially if they feel that the decision didn't take all of the appropriate factors into account. While certainly a long shot, this avenue is open to you and should be taken if there is any indication that the college acted without full information.

If all of your applications are rejected, you should confer immediately with your counselor and map out an alternate course of action. There may be appropriate colleges that are still taking applications, even at this late point in the admission cycle. If you need to strengthen your academic status, you might enroll in a junior or community college or engage in additional preparatory studies and reapply as a transfer applicant.

Many two-year institutions have articulation agreements with four-year colleges and universities where credits are accepted by the senior school and a "seamless" transition occurs whereby the student completes two years at the community college and then continues directly on to a collaborating baccalaureate degree–granting school. Students denied admission should definitely consider this fallback position.

A student receiving acceptance letters should be prepared to inform the one college that he or she wishes to attend of their enrollment decision by May 1, the date viewed by the collegiate community as the universal reply date. Along with your letter of notification, you may be asked to send an admission or housing deposit to confirm your enrollment intentions. Under no circumstances should you declare your intention to enroll at more than one college.

If you're faced with the situation in which you've been accepted to more than one college, you must once again weigh the criteria that you studied in making your application decisions and determine which one of these colleges will present you with the best learning and living situation. When the academic and social scales are even, it may boil down to cost or the financial aid offer, but avoid using these criteria as your primary guide. After letting your new college know that you're accepting their offer of admission, let the others that tendered you an acceptance know of that decision.

Keep your academic work up throughout the remainder of your senior year and begin making plans to be a college freshman. Congratulations. The exploration, decision-making, and application journey is now complete. Exciting times await you at the college that you have just selected!

Frequently Asked Questions

Question: I know where I want to apply. What I don't know is where I will enroll if more than one college accepts me. Can you advise?

Answer: This second decision may be more difficult than the first. Deciding where to enroll means revisiting everything that caused you to consider the college in the first place. If possible, revisit the college, stay overnight, visit a class, eat the food, and live the life of a college student for a day. Concentrate on getting answers to the following three questions. Does it offer the right academic opportunities and promise of success? Will you feel comfortable living on the campus and in the community? Are the college costs, when viewed in light of your family resources and available aid, affordable? Consider the pluses and minuses, and one of the colleges will take center stage. That's where you should enroll.

Question: What can I do if all the colleges I applied to reject me?

Answer: Don't panic! If you thought your application was misinterpreted in any way or that something was overlooked, then you should contact the college. Write a concise letter strongly stating your position and most colleges will gladly give your application a second look. If pleading your case is not an option, confer with your high school counselor and try to determine if any other colleges have freshman vacancies that are compatible with your academic qualifications and personal characteristics. If you need to strengthen your academic status, you may wish to enroll in a community or junior college or engage in some form of remedial study. After you have enhanced your academic background, you can reapply or submit a transfer application in a year or two.

Question: What if more than one college offers me admission and they both want a deposit immediately?

Answer: According to the NACAC Statement of Principles of Good Practice, you have the right to wait until May 1 to respond to any admission and/or financial aid offers. Colleges that request such commitment prior to May 1 must still offer you the opportunity to request an extension (in writing) until May 1. (This right does not apply to early decision candidates.) You can consult the statement at www.nacacnet.org.

Question: How can I improve my chances of admission if I'm placed on a wait-list?

Answer: If you are wait-listed at a college where you would really like to enroll, you first need to determine the typical wait-list movement at the institution. Colleges are usually willing to provide a history (some even include it in your wait-list notification) that describes the number of students wait-listed, the number eventually offered admission, and the availability of financial aid and housing for them. Your potential admission is controlled by the number of acceptances the college receives to its regular offers of admission. You may wish to write a note to the admission office indicating your continued interest in the college. Throughout the process, however, study each of your other options carefully so you have a definite course of action to follow should you not be removed from the wait-list.

Question: I recently heard a student say that her admission letter stated that her acceptance was "conditional." What does that mean?

Answer: By necessity, the admission calendar requires that you submit an application long before you complete high school. In fact, the transcript that accompanies your application will contain grades for only about half of your senior year, less if you have applied under an early decision or early action plan. The college will expect that your final transcript reflect the same level of academic performance after acceptance as before. Some would go so far as to state that your acceptance is "conditional," meaning that your acceptance can be revoked if you fail to maintain your current level of performance.

Question: Once I've been admitted to college, will the admission office really care about my final high school grades and academic record?

Answer: You bet. A serious case of the "senior slump" could have a dramatic effect on your future. The offer of admission is a lot like a contract: a contract with certain contingencies. One such contingency is that you continue your academic performance at a level that justified your acceptance. Why would you want to break stride with a formula that has brought you the reward of college admission? Remember that higher education will make greater demands on you. If you maintain good study habits, you will have an easier time when you begin your college freshman year.

Question: When can I expect the college to ask me and my parents for some money?

Answer: When you receive your offer of admission, just about every college will ask you to submit a housing deposit along with the confirmation that you will be attending their institution. These deposits vary from as low as $250 to as high as $1,000 or more, but that amount is eventually deducted from your freshman year bill. Dorm selection can be tied to the deposit being placed to secure your enrollment and eventual housing location. The remainder of your tuition, room and board, and related costs will be expected closer to the time you register for classes or according to the various payment plans your college might offer.

Student Exercise: 21.1

FROM ADMISSION TO ENROLLMENT: A BRIEF CHECKLIST

College decision making has multiple stages. First, you must decide what colleges to examine. Then you need to decide where to submit applications. The final decision often is the most important. Where will you enroll if accepted? Remember the same criteria that you used when determining where to apply should now be repeated in determining where to enroll.

The following yes/no checklist will allow you to reconsider all of the factors involved in the final selection of your college and may prove useful in pointing you in the right direction.

Enrollment Issues	College A		College B		College C	
	Yes	No	Yes	No	Yes	No
The college has the courses and/or major I want to study.	⎯	⎯	⎯	⎯	⎯	⎯
I am capable of meeting the academic challenges of the college.	⎯	⎯	⎯	⎯	⎯	⎯
The college seems like the right place for me to live and learn.	⎯	⎯	⎯	⎯	⎯	⎯
The community offers the resources (e.g., church, cultural activities, etc.) I will use and enjoy.	⎯	⎯	⎯	⎯	⎯	⎯
The college is affordable.	⎯	⎯	⎯	⎯	⎯	⎯
The financial aid package offered meets my expectations.	⎯	⎯	⎯	⎯	⎯	⎯
_____	⎯	⎯	⎯	⎯	⎯	⎯
_____	⎯	⎯	⎯	⎯	⎯	⎯

CHAPTER 22

Off to College: Getting Ready for Your Freshman Year

The time between graduation in June and starting college in August or September is going to be packed full of more things that need attention than you could have ever imagined. Along with your offer of admission, or soon after you indicate you wish to enroll, your college of choice will begin sending you information that will facilitate the enrollment process.

This information may come from the admission office, the financial aid office, the housing department, and any number of other points of contact on your future campus. Just open these envelopes as they arrive and do everything the college instructs you to do to become fully enrolled.

The months ahead will require that you perform a series of tasks that prepare you to head off to college when summer ends. If you are going to become a residential student, you will be moving to your new college address, a transition that in no small way is like moving from one home to another. Think about all the things that you will require for your relocation and then take the necessary actions.

For example, do you have a checking account now, one that you're going to simply maintain while away at college or are you going to open an account when you get to school. Are there any change-of-address notifications (e.g., magazine subscriptions, etc.) that you need to make? Tasks of this nature require some lead time. Give yourself sufficient time.

Will you need to acquire items (e.g., desk lamps, compact refrigerator, etc.) to make your dorm room more comfortable and functional? Do you have all the learning and study resources (e.g., word-processing software, dictionary, thesaurus, etc.) needed to function away from home? Make the identification or acquisition of these items an all-summer activity and don't leave their collection to the day before you pack the SUV and head down the road.

At some point a couple of weeks before you are to be on campus for freshman orientation, you will need to start assembling and packing your "stuff" and making certain you are fully ready for your move. The farther away you have to travel, the more important this activity becomes, because your parents won't be able to head down to campus one of those early weekends with all the things you forgot.

The final getting ready period should be driven by two lists: a things-to-pack list and a tasks-to-complete list. By working on these two lists over the summer, you'll most likely manage your time and avoid any stress that packing and moving might generate. Many colleges will offer you such a list, including the things that are not permitted (e.g., halogen lighting) in your dorm room. Look for it in your orientation packet.

Unless you're heading off to a very isolated college in a very small community, you will find that a lot of the things you may need can be acquired after you get to school. Even college bookstores have many of the necessities of learning and living, although you may not find them at discount mart prices. And if you forget something personal that you need to have—the U.S. Postal Service, UPS, or FedEx will save the day.

One final summer thought—use these weeks leading up to college to read and write and engage in academic pursuits (formal summer workshops or classes, or informal Internet experiences) that further prepare you for the challenges you are about to undertake. Anything you do to strengthen your skills as a future college student will pay huge dividends.

Upon getting to college, be sure to participate in any orientation programs offered to you. These programs are designed to educate you about the college, its programs and services, and all of the "nuts and bolts" you need to know in order to launch a successful learning and living experience. Since orientation programs are often scheduled a few days before the campus is in full operation, they permit you to meet other students and learn about the institution in a casual and stress-free environment. Once classes start, develop your personal routine and become aware of all of the resources (people, services, etc.) positioned in various parts of the student service department. These people and programs can help you get off to and maintain a positive college experience.

Frequently Asked Questions

Question: What control do I have over the selection of my roommate and what can be done if we don't get along?

Answer: For most students, college represents the first real independent living experience and that includes meeting new people and learning to live in a different social environment. Roommate compatibility is created through openness, honesty, and a willingness to understand each other's needs, likes and dislikes, habits, and other characteristics. Roommate problems occur when balance and reciprocity are missing. You can get off to the best start by completing roommate contracts and questionnaires honestly. This information will be used by housing officers in making room assignments. Attempt to resolve differences through negotiation and adjustment, not confrontation. Should you find yourself in a situation that is difficult to resolve, the college may be able to accommodate your (or your roommate's) need to move to another room.

Question: How can I survive the college workload?

Answer: The key to meeting college workload requirements is good time management. Begin while you are still in high school to develop these skills and make the most of the time you designate for tasks like reading, general study, research and writing assignments, and exam preparation. Identify the "time bandits" (e.g., interruptions, procrastination, telephone calls) and determine ways of avoiding or dealing with them. Have the tools and resources necessary to do your work nearby or go to the location (e.g., library, computer center) where they are available. Try creating a time budget or schedule. Determine in advance how long a task will take and stick to it. Over time, discipline and experience will produce the desired results.

Question: What resources exist at the college to help me if I experience difficulty with my studies?

Answer: Most colleges provide tutoring, mentoring, and related programs to help students who have difficulty meeting their academic obligations. Typically found in the office of student affairs or student development, these programs can only be useful if you don't wait too long before going for help. As soon as you recognize you're having trouble, talk with your professor to determine what he or she might recommend to get you back on track. If you require more intensive or long-term assistance, be certain to get in touch with the student affairs office.

Student Exercise 22.1

MOVING ON: PACKING FOR COLLEGE

Following is a generic checklist of items that students have identified as necessary for their study and lifestyle needs. The list should not be considered exhaustive. Your personal needs and tastes will dictate what you place on your personal list.

Study Items

_____ Calculator
_____ Computer with printer
_____ Dictionary/thesaurus/writing guide
_____ Recorder and cassettes
_____ Software

_____ _____
_____ _____
_____ _____

Desk Items

_____ Batteries (various sizes)
_____ Bookends
_____ Calendar
_____ Cords (phone and electric)
_____ File folders/notebooks
_____ Index/note cards/sticky notes
_____ Paper
_____ Pens/pencils/markers/highlighters
_____ Ruler
_____ Scissors
_____ Stamps
_____ Stapler
_____ Stationery/envelopes
_____ Tacks/tapes/paper clips/rubber bands/magnets
_____ Tool set (small)

_____ _____
_____ _____
_____ _____

Entertainment Items

_____ Camera and film
_____ Playing cards/games
_____ Radio/cassette player/CD player, headset/headphones
_____ Sporting equipment (e.g., bike, football, Frisbee, tennis racket, etc.)
_____ Television

_____ _____
_____ _____
_____ _____

Room Items

_____ Alarm clock
_____ Bedding (sheets, pillowcases, mattress cover)
_____ Bottle opener
_____ Bulletin board (small)
_____ Clamp-on lamp (for bed reading)
_____ Coffeemaker
_____ Cordless phone/answering machine
_____ Desk lamp
_____ First aid kit/Band-Aids (assorted sizes)
_____ Flashlight
_____ Hangers
_____ Iron
_____ Laundry bag/basket and detergent
_____ Mirror (hand)
_____ Mugs, dishes, and utensils
_____ Pillows/cushions
_____ Posters, pictures, and room decorations
_____ Refrigerator (3.6 cubic feet or smaller)
_____ Sewing kit
_____ Towels and washcloths
_____ Throw rug(s)
_____ Trash and storage bags
_____ Underbed storage boxes/storage crates
_____ Wastebasket (extra)

_____ _____
_____ _____
_____ _____

Clothing Items

_____ Athletic wear/swimsuit
_____ Bathrobe (bathroom isn't as close as home)
_____ Clothing (seasonal)
_____ Clothing (multiseasonal—if you won't be getting home)
_____ Flip-flops or shower shoes
_____ Foul weather gear
_____ Special event apparel (for when jeans aren't appropriate)
_____ _____
_____ _____

Personal Items

_____ Hairbrush/dryer
_____ Medications, pain relievers/vitamins
_____ Soaps, shampoos, and toiletries
_____ Toothbrush, toothpaste, floss, etc.
_____ Shower caddy/bath tote/soap case
_____ _____
_____ _____

Miscellaneous Items

_____ Backpack
_____ Glasses/contacts (extra set)
_____ Checkbook
_____ Credit card/ATM card
_____ Purchasing card (general merchandise, office supply, and/or hardware stores)
_____ Driver's license/passport/Social Security card
_____ Fan
_____ Insurance cards
_____ Luggage/trunk
_____ Plants
_____ Umbrella
_____ Battery charger
_____ _____
_____ _____

Items you will typically find provided

Bed/mattress
Desk/desk chair
Dresser/closet
Phone (standard)
Wastebasket and recycling bin

Items not allowed or requiring prior approval

Appliances with open heating elements
Candles
Halogen lights
Hot plates

CHAPTER 23

Parents and the High School-to-College Transition

The period of time when students are considering their college options and making decisions about the future is filled with excitement, discovery, and sometimes a feeling of being overwhelmed. There is much to be learned and many tasks to complete. Like all of the schooling experiences that preceded it, this is a time for parental support and involvement.

Parental participation can ensure that the student engages in effective exploration and carries out the planning and application tasks in a thorough and efficient manner. Parents can help their children formulate relevant questions and analyze the information that is gathered in response. They can also lessen the anxiety and confusion that often finds its way into the college admission process.

General Educational Guidance

Much of the parental role during the final years of high school must be directed toward the general educational experience, making certain that the student is engaged in studies that are consistent with his or her abilities, aptitudes, interests, and accomplishments.

Parents can also help their child in the development of effective study and time management skills and make certain he or she has the tools and materials to do an effective job as a student. They must also create an atmosphere or climate that encourages curiosity and discovery and promotes reading, experimentation, and expression.

The parent should work with teachers and counselors to track the child's learning experiences and address any issues or problems that could result in the student not realizing his or her full learning potential.

College Guidance

The second parental guidance role deals directly with the college exploration, decision-making, and application process.

First, parents should help their sons and daughters understand the reasons why they are going to college and aid them in the formulation of educational and career goals. This will entail the appraisal of personal abilities, aptitudes, and interests and relating what they learn about themselves to the educational and career options before them.

This is a time to respect the individuality of children and the fact that they are still growing and maturing. Parents must also respect their children's right to make decisions about their personal future. Parents must be careful to remember who is going to college and whose life is being planned.

The student who plays a major role in the decisions that affect her or his future has a greater investment in making those decisions work. It is easier to fail or have mediocre success at the decisions that others make or force upon you. Parents should recognize the difference between guiding and steering. Guiding is an opening, promoting, and supporting parental behavior. Steering is a controlling, dominating, and insulating one.

Parents can be active participants in the college exploration and admission process. They should visit campuses with their child and participate in the parent programs offered by admission offices. Supportive parents help the child acquire and evaluate the information needed to make good decisions. Parents should (1) make certain the student has been thorough in his or her search by studying the same publications, websites, and related resources; (2) review the admission and financial aid applications and offer information or guidance in their completion; (3) make certain that tasks get completed and forms are submitted on time; and (4) be the calming force when confusion and anxiety enter the picture.

Career Guidance

Parents in the workplace or with career experiences can be incredibly valuable sources of information for the student explorer and decision maker. Parents can provide opportunities for their sons and daughters to learn both formally (i.e., visits to the workplace, volunteer roles, etc.) and informally (i.e., chats and discussions about their occupations and careers) about the workplace.

Above all, parents need to be proud, loving, and encouraging, and help a son or daughter deal with the outcome of the quest for college admission. When this experience has ended, they'll be the parents of a college freshman.

Frequently Asked Questions

Question: My parents want to be involved with my college decision. How can I keep them from taking over?

Answer: Your parents probably want to be involved because they care about you and your future. Make sure they know about your goals and aspirations, what you want to study, and the career or careers you feel are best suited for you. Keep them informed regarding your exploration and let them know that you are on course. Many parents jump into the process because they feel their son or daughter isn't accepting the responsibility. Avoid "parental takeover" by showing that you're in control.

CHAPTER 24

Educational Success: How Counselors Can Help You

The school counselor can be one of your greatest allies during the years that you are in high school. Unfortunately, many students fail to utilize the services of the counseling staff or participate in the programs they offer in support of their education. Others wait too long to make the counselor connection.

Consider your counselor to be a specialist, a person specifically trained to help you make the most of your educational experience and plan for your future education, career, and life. Counselors work with all students, not just those who are experiencing problems or difficulty. The terms used to describe the two basic types of counseling assistance are *preventative* and *remedial*.

Preventative assistance means a counselor can assist you in the orderly progression through school and the various educational, social, and emotional situations you will encounter. Remedial assistance is offered by the counselor when you need to address problems and resolve conflicts that stand between you and your success in school and in life.

As you progress through school, you will be faced with numerous opportunities to interact with the counselor to gather information, address concerns or problems, and set goals for the future. In many ways, your specific counseling needs may be identical to those of your peers. After all, you and your classmates are experiencing the trials and joys of adolescence and young adulthood.

Some of your counseling needs, however, may be different or unique to your personal learning and living situation. Your counselor is prepared to assist you in the confidential treatment of these special concerns.

Counselor assistance can take many forms. Sometimes one-on-one interaction between the student and counselor produces the desired outcomes. In other situations, a counselor might choose to interact with a group of students. And, in other cases, the counselor may visit the classroom or conduct a special seminar to provide information that you and your fellow students might require. Finally, your counselor may serve as a "middle" person, gathering information from you, your parents, and your teachers and bringing everything together in a manner that works best for you and your future. Counselors are trained and prepared to help you in the ways specified below:

- Monitoring academic achievement and assisting you in the selection of courses during high school.
- Diagnosing learning difficulties and recommending corrective measures.
- Evaluating study habits and offering suggestions on how to improve them.
- Administering tests and interpreting results.
- Assisting you in the appraisal and understanding of your aptitudes, abilities, achievements, and interests.
- Counseling you regarding future education and career options and providing information that promotes exploration and leads to sound decision making.

A good counselor–student relationship is dependent upon trust, open communication, and mutual acceptance. Your counselor will guide, not steer, you toward a greater understanding and realization of your full educational potential and show you ways to strengthen your classroom performance. Don't ask or expect your counselor to make your decisions for you.

Your counselor can help you best if he or she has a good understanding of your abilities, aptitudes, interests, and achievements. Get to know your counselor early in the high school experience and return for assistance as frequently as personal needs dictate. The result can be improved academic achievement and enhanced options for your future. Make that appointment today!

CHAPTER 25

School to College: Counselors as Your Allies

As you consider educational opportunities after high school, there are a number of experts available to help you gather information, examine options, make decisions, apply for admission and financial aid, and move from high school-to-college. Seize every opportunity to benefit from their expertise and guidance. You won't regret it.

School Counselors

While you're in high school, especially during the junior and senior years, counselors can perform the following functions to aid you in the school-to-college transition:

- Conduct individual and group counseling sessions that help you

    identify learning objectives,
    understand the mission of different colleges and universities,
    examine colleges that are compatible with your academic, financial, and lifestyle
        requirements,
    evaluate information and make decisions,
    deal with acceptance and rejection of your college application,
    prepare for life as a college freshman, and
    relate educational exploration and decision making to your personal career de-
        velopment.

- Provide information (publications, videos, Internet websites, etc.) about colleges and other postsecondary education opportunities.
- Sponsor college fairs and similar events and host college representatives in an
effort to expose you to quality human resources.

- Offer guidance on how to complete college applications and financial aid forms and prepare for campus visits, admission tests, and application essays.
- Send transcripts, letters of recommendation, and school profiles to colleges in support of your application.
- Offer information and assistance to parents.

Admission and Financial Aid Counselors

Counselors and admission officers at the college and university level are also equipped to aid you in this very important selection and transition process. An admission officer once suggested that the women and men who work in college admission programs should be viewed as "path lighters," not "gatekeepers." This is wise advice.

Admission officers want to attract students to their institution. But they want to recruit the "right" students: individuals who will enroll, succeed, and graduate at the end of the collegiate experience. Their role is not one of prohibiting or denying, but rather of promoting access to those students with the abilities, achievements, and interests that are required to experience success at their college or university.

Any questions that you have about the college, its educational programs, student life, or the application process should be directed to the attention of an admission counselor. Don't make application until you get the answers.

Financial aid counselors and administrators have a similar mission. They work to help you understand college costs and the financial assistance that is available to you and your family. Once they have defined your level of need, they will identify all resources (e.g., grants, scholarships, loans, work-study programs) for which you may be eligible.

These college and university representatives can also guide you through the seemingly endless forms that are required to apply for admission and financial aid.

In utilizing the services of any of these counselors, be sensitive to time constraints and calendar demands. Your needs will receive maximum attention if you establish early and ongoing contact and if you don't place impossible demands on the counselor. Help your counselors help you in the school-to-college transition.

Frequently Asked Questions

Question: What are the rewards and risks of hiring an independent, fee-charging counselor or consultant?

Answer: Private counselors have a limited caseload and can offer more individualized attention than that offered by school counselors, especially if you haven't engaged in the progressive consideration of your options, gathering of information, and related admission and financial aid tasks. Expect to pay fees that may run $1,000 to $2,500 or more for these services. Like test preparation programs and scholarship services, you're encouraged to exhaust all existing programs and services before you ask your parents to get out the checkbook.

If you decide to consult with an independent counselor, first ask him or her for a list of references that you can check before you make a financial commitment. Make certain the independent counselor is reputable and don't be afraid to ask them for an agreement that outlines the services to be provided. You should also obtain a copy of *Counseling, Test Prep and Financial Aid Services: A Consumer's Guide*, a free brochure from the National Association for College Admission Counseling, 1050 N. Highland Street, Suite 400, Arlington, VA 22201. The Independent Educational Consultants Association (IECA) represents experienced professionals who provide college counseling. You can consult their membership directory at www.educationalconsulting.org/.

Question: On several occasions I've asked my counselor to recommend the best colleges for me, but she seems reluctant to do so. Why?

Answer: It sounds like your counselor is a believer in the theory that the student needs to be involved in the exploration and decision-making process and, thereby, become responsible for his or her choices. The role of the counselor in the college guidance process is to guide, not steer, and to help you take a realistic look at educational options in light of your abilities, achievements, and future goals. Expect your counselor to be supportive and to inform, motivate, and clarify, but ultimately, you must choose the colleges to which you will apply and the college where you will enroll.

Question: Many fee-charging services say they can help you gain college admission and/or financial aid. Are they worth trying?

Answer: Before considering any private service, I recommend that the first resource you turn to is yourself. The admission and financial aid process requires your personal attention. As you get involved in the process, you will find that many resources are available to you free through your counseling office, library, and the colleges themselves. The counselors in your school and in the various college admission and financial aid offices are ready to assist you. Use these resources before you turn to any fee-charging services.

Student Exercise 25.1

TRACKING COUNSELING SESSIONS AND FOLLOW-UP TASKS

In the space below, record notes of your counseling sessions and any follow-up tasks you must perform.

Date	Notes and Follow-up Tasks	Completed

CHAPTER 26

Some Closing Words about Expectations

The key to successful college decision making is effective exploration. Take a long look at yourself, your aptitudes, abilities, interests, and past achievements. Set realistic educational goals and then mount the most thorough examination of options you can orchestrate.

The philosophy of this book is that there are multiple colleges that are "right" for you and your search should be focused on identifying as many of them as possible. That will not always mean your first choice or the one your parents want you to attend. It won't likely be the one your best friend has selected. It means a college that is good for you and a lot of dynamics will interplay as the discovery runs its course.

You get to choose what colleges to examine and the ones to which you will direct applications. The colleges, on the other hand, get to look at your academic qualifications, life experiences, and your personal characteristics and determine if they match up with those established for future students. It is indeed a very dynamic process.

A few words about expectations are appropriate here. Expect to work hard during the entire exploration and decision-making process. Expect to work even harder when you begin to apply to colleges and universities, especially when the number of applications you submit is three or greater.

Expect the colleges to be interested in you. The more "admissible" you are—the more interest they will show in you. In other words, the more you mirror the profile of the student they want on their campus, the more they will do to court you and try to get you to enroll. Finally, expect to be treated in a fair and ethical manner and complain when you feel this is not the case.

Don't expect colleges where you don't fit the profile to be as interested. They will be courteous, but clear in their view that you don't possess the academic and personal qualifications they seek. And don't expect them to bend just because it is you.

Don't expect the admission formula that colleges use to remain the same from year to year. The admission recipe ingredients will likely be constant, but the emphasis may shift as colleges seek to create the student body they want to have. Finally, don't expect to know the "why" about how you were accepted for enrollment or denied admission. Some things about this whole process will be a total mystery and defy explanation.

Hopefully the *Bound-for-College Guidebook*, with all of its information and exercises will light the path to a number of colleges that will help you achieve your educational and career ambitions. Those are the colleges where you should submit applications. At the end of this exciting and sometimes tedious process, you will be in a good place—most likely the right place. You will be a college freshman.

About the Author

Dr. **Frank Burtnett** is a veteran counselor, teacher, education association officer, and consultant who currently serves as president of Education Now, an educational consulting, research, and resource development firm located in Springfield, Virginia, and Rockport, Maine. Over his career, Frank served as the executive director/CEO of the National Association for College Admission Counseling and associate executive director of the American Counseling Association.

He is the author of the *Parent's Guide to the College Admission Process*, a publication of the National Association for College Admission Counseling, and developed the Beta College Guidance Center and Beta Career Guidance Center, two innovative Internet-based information banks used by the more than 240,000 student members of the National Beta Club. He coauthored the AT&T publication, *Selecting the Right College*, which has been distributed to more than one million students nationally. He also wrote and edited numerous college and career guidance pieces for the *Careers & Colleges* and *Futures* magazines and the Family Education Network. He conducts interactive webinars for parents, educators, and members of such groups at the National Institute of Certified College Planners.

Currently, Frank serves as an adjunct professor on the counselor education faculty of the School of Education and Human Services of Marymount University in Arlington, Virginia. He has also developed and presented seminars on educational and career development topics for numerous institution, agency, organization, and private sector sponsors. He is a popular speaker at both professional and public programs.

Frank holds a Bachelor of Science degree in education from Shippensburg University (Pennsylvania) and Master of Arts and Doctor of Education degrees from George Washington University (Washington, D.C.) and has earned the National Certified Counselor and National Certified Career Counselor credentials of the National Board for Certified Counselors and the Master Career Counselor certificate of the National Career Development Association. He is a registered counselor (RC2478) in the state of Maine.